Riesling

Christina Fischer, Ingo Swoboda

Riesling

The full diversity of the world's noblest vine

With photographs by Robert Dieth

Translated by Jon Smale

 Hallwag

RIESLING PASSION

A many-voiced anthem

Hans-Günther Schwarz, wine producer

In an outstanding manner, this gift of nature characterizes our understanding of wine culture. Riesling can likewise convey the fascination of the moment as well as being a symbol for a nature-oriented attitude of mind. The perfect harmony of berriness, fruit, acidity and minerality opens up unique experiences of taste. In this way, the pleasure of wine takes on significance and the highest aspiration.

Harald Rüssel,
Landhaus St. Urban,
Jeunes Restaurateurs d'Europe, Germany

There is a number of good reasons why I so gladly cook for or with Riesling: our Landhaus St. Urban is situated in a valley of a tributary of the Mosel, my wife comes from a Riesling estate, but above all Riesling has characteristics which suit cuisine marvelously. This is due to the acidity structure of Rieslings, even in their off-dry range, which can buffer tanginess and, through their complexity, leave behind lingering aroma sensations upon the tongue and above all on the palate. If one builds bridges for Riesling between the individual components of a dish, then it will cut a fine figure for almost all foods.

Kazuo Hoshino,
wine merchant, Tokyo

For me, Riesling is like the leader of an orchestra who is outstandingly proficient with his instrument, but nevertheless requires a conductor. If the winemaker succeeds as conductor to find the right cue, then the Riesling can interrelate with the acidity like a virtuoso. This fine acidity interplay is ever more interesting with time, and it is unique. Riesling possesses a fascinating expressiveness which varies according to climate, soil, harvesting date and the winemaker's method of processing. In Japan, Riesling is considered as the best white grape variety. However, it is not easy for the Japanese consumer to find the right flavor. Charta, Classic, Selection, Grosses Gewächs – there are too many appellations. That is the biggest problem of German wine.

Dr. Josef Schuller, MW,
Wine Academy Rust, Austria

Riesling is the world's greatest and most valuable white variety. No other type of grape is so able to convey the magic of wine as Riesling does: the character, the origin, the country, the soil, the climate, the vintage, in short – the terroir. One can taste, smell and feel it with Riesling as with no other grape variety. It enchants in its youth through its lively, animating freshness and entices in its maturity via characteristic grandeur. Hitherto the classical, cool cultivation regions of Europe have been able to assert themselves in the face of competition from abroad – they are actually in a different league. However, particularly the new Rieslings from the cool regions of the world demonstrate to us that the search for the holy grail of white wine is in full swing.

Jancis Robinson, MW, London

Riesling is the greatest white wine grape in the world.

Michel Bettane, wine journalist, France

I have considered Riesling to be the noblest of the white wine varieties for a long time. Its noblesse becomes equally apparent in the wines as in the vine itself, and I have always admired the proud habitus and the special form of the small bunches with their finely veined grapes. I value Riesling mainly for two reasons: with unparalleled clarity, it demonstratively expresses even the finest distinctions of terroir and it requires no oak aging at all in order to achieve more character. Riesling permits dry whites to be created as well as medium and sweet growths that without doubt rank with the world's best. I am very pleased about Riesling now winning back its well-earned worldwide top position.

Peter Gago, chief winemaker, Southcorp, Australia

Riesling is the distinctive grape variety which evokes a passion in winemakers and connoisseurs of the finest wines. Riesling's purity and elegance embraces the senses with pristine clarity, and it tantalizes with a paradoxical complexity and an expressive versatility. The essence of this passion is the selective nature of this grape variety to succinctly express the unique typicity of the vineyard terroir and the season in which the fruit was formed. Riesling, of all grape varieties, can best provide a snap shot of time and place. It is a looking glass which accurately reflects and exposes the naked splendor of any given vineyard and vintage.

Terry Theise, wine merchant, USA

Riesling is exceptional because if you grow it where it's at home, it comes out of the ground already perfect. It doesn't need any face-lift, depilating, tummy-tucks or pancake makeup, not like a certain other variety one could name. Riesling knows soil more intimately than any other grape, and is more articulate than any other grape in conveying soil right onto your quivering palate. Riesling attracts the kinds of vintners who do not need to prove to you what big deals they are by how well they can diddle technology. With Riesling, nature rules. In the cellar, less is more. Riesling survives frost, because it ripens late in the Fall when everything is taut and crisp and golden. Its wines are the afterglow of the contented world.

Markus del Monego, MW, World's Best Sommelier 1998

Riesling is fascinating. In the cool, climatic border area it has an almost unlimited potential, whereas in regions with a warmer climate it can mutate into a one-dimensional drink. Riesling is modern. Due to its fine, somewhat refreshingly crisp acidity, its impressively stark fruit and usually delightfully integrated minerality, it has become a perfect accompaniment to worldwide trends in cuisine. Riesling is irreplaceable. For this reason I always have a Riesling in my luggage on my travels through the world of wine.

CONTENTS

ABOUT THIS BOOK

To devote an entire book to a single grape variety is a difficult and perhaps also a daring endeavor, above all when it is about a grape variety which is not one of the global players but is nonetheless popular. Along with Chardonnay, Sauvignon Blanc and Muscat, Riesling is considered one of the world's four classic white grape varieties. Despite its worldwide minimal share of four percent, it is found in almost all cultivation regions of the international world of wine, perhaps sporadically, as a decorative complement to a particular selection, or even as a showpiece. In some areas it is the main grape variety and for some producers it is a serious experiment or simply a hobby. However, for many wine producers Riesling is a part of their life and requires, along with the oft-mentioned terroir, healthy ambition, experience, and above all passion.

It is not the intention of this book to evaluate and to compare Riesling with other white wines. Rather, this book is intended to offer the reader a comprehensive insight into the multifaceted world of Riesling and to stimulate him or her to discover and experience this diversity of taste. It is difficult to impart, even in a wine book like this, how good Riesling can be. It remains an individual question of taste, even though balance and harmony are certainly quite objective criteria for the quality of a wine.

Since sampling – thankfully – comes before studying, we recommend to you wines from the entire world of Riesling for "self-study". They are our personal favorites which in no way lay claim to be the wisdom and the last word on Riesling. This also applies to the addresses at the end of this book. In order for you to quickly find your Riesling type or your flavor-favorites, we have arranged the wines not alphabetically by country, region or producer, but by flavor type and Riesling-characteristics.

We now wish you, not a dry recitation, but a refreshing and enjoyable read about all aspects of Riesling.

Christina Fischer & Ingo Swoboda

WHY RIESLING?

Opinions differ considerably with Riesling. As a grape variety it is a hazardous venture, a balancing act during the ripening period of a grape and at the same time a challenge to the craft skills of the winemaker, and to the palate of the consumer. Riesling is easy to underestimate. However, it can produce not only long-lived wines, but like no other, exhibits the characteristics of its origin without giving up its identity or typicity.

Riesling challenges. It reveals itself in its full glory only to those who are not contented with their first sip. Riesling is attractive, but can at the same time be dismissive until one pays it the full attention that it demands of itself.

The strength of Riesling lies in the encounter of fine, elegant nuances and the multifacetedness of the various aromas. In addition, there is the dance-like play of the sometimes quite pungent acidity that reveals finesse and the desired brilliance. The contradictory quality in its character is that particular range of dry to noble-sweet which Riesling unfolds in its long vegetation and ripening period. Herein, certainly, lies a reason for the myth that surrounds this grape variety and makes it so attractive and delightful.

Over the last few years, the wine world has spoken of a Riesling renaissance, and it appears that its discovery by the New World is in no way a mere fashion trend following in the path of the global wine circus. Certainly, no other white grape with low alcoholic content offers so much diversity and varied facets of flavor. Herein lies the excitement of Riesling. It is nevertheless not suited to everyone's taste, and – notably thanks to its vegetative predilection for cool climate zones and the consequently limited availability of cultivation areas – only with difficulty can it be forced into the tight constraints of an assumed "popular" flavor.

Riesling puts up resistance. Looked at thus, it is perhaps a relic from an old wine and flavor world, a reminiscence of the traditional craft skills of the winemaker's handiwork, and of the consideration that for centuries, viticulture meant individual agriculture, that is, a give-and-take by man and nature in what was ultimately an unpredictable relationship of dependence, with an unknown outcome, but above all with individual traits.

Particularly in a world which is economically inexorably coalescing, and thereby losing its local peculiarities and specialties little by little in favor of compromise products oriented to mass consumption, Riesling is always a good bet for a surprise. It has personality, character and passion. Hence Riesling!

WHAT IS A GREAT RIESLING?

The question is justifiable, but not easy to answer. Quite the contrary. For although many wine-lovers have certainly already drunk so-called great Rieslings, or know of their prestigious names and appellations, it depends – as so often in life – upon the perspective from which one answers the question. A question of taste? Perhaps.

VARYING ASPECTS

If one asks the wine producer, then at the inception of a great Riesling we have first of all first-class grapes from a special location, and the idea of the producer to create a great wine from it. For the marketing specialist on the other hand, terroir, estate and élevage are only means to an end: namely to achieve as high a price as possible. Many wine-lovers on the other hand peer harder than ever at the published opinion of (supposed) experts who appraise and assess wines.

Furthermore, the oenologist should ideally bring together all these aspects into a wine, in order to guarantee its success. An impossible task? Perhaps.

NATIONAL PECULIARITIES

Yet, what distinguishes a great Riesling? In Germany one would firstly name the varietal character that should perfectly embody and unite in a wine all that which distinguishes a Riesling. In Alsace the winemaker would above all call for a particularly distinct characteristic of the terroir, since from his quality considerations only particularly favorable locations are suitable for the production of great Rieslings. An American on the other hand would consider complexity to be the highest criterion, that is, the intricacy of Riesling that brings as many as possible individual olfactory and gustatory components together into a fascinating whole, and an Australian would promote the flavor which the consumer expects, so that the wine can be established as a brand.

INDIVIDUAL PREFERENCES

According to how one defines a great Riesling, there arise very varied consequences as to how to attain this objective. While the American would choose to ferment a Riesling with a high degree of turbidity in order to increase body and suppleness, and in malolactic fermentation, in order to achieve an increase in complexity, the German would be apprehensive of masking the varietal character with a buttery tinge that results from malolactic fermentation. A French winemaker would never allow the mixing of a number of terroirs and would castigate it as a cultural disgrace, while Australian winemakers would describe

The composition of the soil can influence the flavor quality of a wine

this as a suitable method of increasing the complexity of the wine.

In contrast, the French winemaker chaptalizes his principal wines without compunction, while German winemakers with their Prädikat wines are proud of being able to obtain maturity solely from the grapes. Conversely, high acidity concentrations are also part of the French terroir thinking and are not regulated, while German winemakers have learnt through intelligent acidity management to counterbalance the harshest fluctuations of nature and thereby to produce more digestible wines. What is then ultimately a great Riesling?

THIS IS A GREAT RIESLING

Ulrich Fischer, professor of winemaking and oenology in Neustadt an der Weinstrasse, has put it in a nutshell:

"A great Riesling exudes a maximum of typicity of the grape variety, coupled with the noticeable influence of the location. Both these aspects should lastingly reveal themselves through a special diversity of aromas and flavor impressions and facilitate a high storage potential. The first-class quality of a great Riesling should be apparent and meet with approval, while its quite individual as well as authentic sensory particularity is not expected to please everyone."

HISTORY AND WINEMAKING

THE DEMANDS OF THE RIESLING VARIETY

CULTURE-DEFINING

Riesling over the centuries

It may be that from today's viewpoint the historical traces of Riesling appear only as marginal notes in history. However, history is also a justification for developments and the decisions resulting from them, which enable new things to appear by making changes to old things. The decision for Riesling and thereby also for its peculiarities as an agricultural crop has lastingly shaped and influenced landscapes, set courses for cultural change and alongside the monastic wine culture – to which many famous locations can be traced back – also allowed the growth of a rural social structure which is associated with Riesling to the present day. And over the generations Riesling has influenced taste, even if the variety has been modified time and again through biological options. Taste, as we know, is not genetically defined. There is a causal relationship between it, the natural and man-made conditions of a landscape and a culture, and the resulting interpretation and mediation of learning.

UNCERTAIN PROVENANCE

As with the majority of grape varieties, the provenance of Riesling too has been speculated upon time and again. Alsace – Riesling was mentioned in writing for the first time during a visit by Duke René II of Lorraine in 1477 – as well as Germany claim to be its home. Thus, a certain myth surrounds Riesling from the very beginning. Some scholars claim to recognize Riesling in a variety already mentioned by the Roman writer Pliny the Elder. Others see King Louis the German (804–876) as the person who had the vine planted in the Rhineland, and yet other experts presume Riesling to be a variation of a wild Germanic vine; *vitis vinifera silvestris.* Even the origin of the name is unclear. It probably dates from the 15th century and could be derived from Russling (rus = dark wood) but equally well from Rissling (rissig = to tear).

WHITE INSTEAD OF RED

The winegrowing lexicon of 1930 says quite clearly under the heading 'Riesling': "Native habitat: Germany. Probably a seedling from the Rheingau." The reason for this assumption appears to be that in the Rheingau in 1392 white grapes were being planted alongside the previously dominant black varieties. The Cistercian abbey in Eberbach actually enforced this "white movement" and demanded of its tenants that they plant white grapes. Apparently the monks had problems with their produce – at the then-important Cologne wine market – and could not successfully assert themselves over the red-wine competition from their Burgundian brethren.

The way out of the dilemma was seen in the offer of a very convincing white wine, typical of the region. Whether it was a Riesling is not

The Eberbach Cistertian abbey in the Rheingau region is considered the birthplace of German wine culture

recorded, but it may be assumed. For, on a winery bill of March 13, 1435 addressed to the counts of Katzenelnbogen, who had their family tomb at Eberbach Abbey, there is a reference to "seczreben riesslingen in die wingarten."

MONASTERIES PREFER "RISSLING"

In its present day spelling, the grape variety is mentioned for the first time in 1552 in a Latin text of the herbal of Hieronymus Bock. The German edition of 1577 states: "Rieslinge wachsen an der Mosel, am Rhein und im Wormser Gau." (Rieslings grow at the Mosel, at the Rhine and in the Worms district.) However, before the variety could assert itself, bad harvests, peasants' revolts and the Thirty Years' War slowed down the upturn in the wine industry in all parts of Europe. Only from the mid-17th century onwards did endeavors begin regarding the qualitative improvement of winemaking and at the same time the triumphal advance of Riesling. Thus, St. Clare's monastery in Mainz decreed in 1672 that the black-grape vines are to be cut out and replaced with good "Rissling-wood". The cultivation of the hitherto popular white

RIESLING
HISTORY AND WINEMAKING

Elbling was proscribed. In 1695 the St. Maximin monastery at Grünhaus on the Ruwer had new vines planted, and we can presume that they included Riesling vines.

In 1720, 294,000 vines were planted in the vineyards of the old Benedictine abbey of Johannisberg, which was now subordinated to the Prince Abbot of Fulda: of these the "Rissling" was of foremost importance. Truly an initial spark which prompted the last cellarer of Fulda Abbey, Odo Staab, to note: "In the entire Rheingau no other variety of grape is allowed to be planted for the making of wines, excepting that of Rüsslinge." To this day, in some winegrowing regions of the New World the name "Johannisberger" can be found as a synonym for Riesling.

A VINE OF ALL CLASSES

Gradually, decrees from spiritual landlords and the founding of new monasteries and monastery farmlands ensured the introduction and diffusion of Riesling from the Mosel down to the Rhine, and from Alsace into the Wachau valley. On January 11, 1744 the prince-bishop of Speyer, Cardinal Franz Christoph von Hutten, decreed for his Deidesheim territory: Elbling is no longer to be cultivated, but rather more noble varieties and among them the Riesling.

In Alsace in 1756, the Jesuit college in Schlettstadt had Riesling planted, and the Elector Archbishop of Trier, Clemens Wenceslaus, ordered by decree of May 8, 1787, "All inferior varieties of grape are to be cut down and replaced by Riesling." Alongside ecclesiastical possessions and those of the nobility there existed however a bourgeois viticulture, which was in the hands either of municipalities or of individual wealthy merchants and landowners.

MONASTIC INNOVATION

Nevertheless, it was above all the monasteries that remained the driving force for innovations in winemaking technology, and also for research and the scientific consideration of wine making. In the 18th century, the proportion of income due to winemaking of the Eberbach monastery in Rheingau already amounted to about 50%. From the idea of protecting oneself against the risks of bad vintages by retaining selected good wines, there arose here, under the name "cabinet," a separate cellar storage. The term was established at the beginning of the 18th century and was assigned in Schloss Vollrads to particularly high-quality wines. In 1775 the former Johannisberg monastery discovered "Spätlese" or "late harvest"; a monument in the courtyard of the present-day palace recalls this event. Indeed, chroniclers report that already by 1730, some winemakers "readily await a little rotting, in order to attain a greater sweetness of the grapes," and in 1753 and 1760, from rotten Steinberger grapes in Eberbach monastery "a particularly good batch of wine" was pressed. Nevertheless 1775 remains the date that marks the beginning of a methodical and specifically spät (late) lese (picking) of noble-rot grapes.

It was particularly the sweet Rieslings which earned renown and image for the grape variety in all of Europe, and were never found lacking at the royal, imperial, czarist or princely table. These wines were served at the midday meal as well as during the formal evening dinner, on an equal footing with Champagnes and great clarets. It was above all the heyday of the German Rieslings, which, up to the beginning of the 20th century, together with the white and red Burgundies and red Bordeaux wines, made up the quartet of the most famous and most expensive wines in the world.

THE NATIVE VINEYARD

The green world of Riesling

A wine is born in the vineyard, where it literally has its roots, and the soil with its geological, geographical and climatological characteristics represents the "wine homeland". A main focus of work in the vineyard is the preservation of the health of the soil, which partly determines the character of the taste. The growth of the vines is at the same time the hour of birth of quality, which the winegrower can support and influence via a vineyard management suited to local peculiarities. Only what arrives for processing in the cellar can be exploited during vinification and thereby retained for the future wine. No winemaker can make good wine from poor-quality grapes.

Riesling, as a late-ripening variety, finds in the relatively cool cultivation zones around the 49th to the 51st parallels of the northern hemisphere the climatic conditions that can bring the little grapes to express their intensive flavor and full maturity.

The vegetation period of at least 100 days after flowering (on a ten-year average between June 15 and 25) is prolonged to up to 130 days by many Riesling growers in order to give the grapes additional ripening time on the vine and thus the possibility of a more intensive accumulation of aroma.

CORRECTLY SITUATED?

Although Riesling can endure a relatively cool climate, it prefers sheltered locations if it is to achieve full ripeness and produce commercial yields. The hardy vine demonstrates its quality above all on relatively barren terrain such as stony residual soils. However, pure south-facing slopes do not in themselves create the better vineyards. To a greater degree, the prolonged evening sunshine on slopes inclined to the south-west offers the grapes the chance to slowly develop their aroma structure. The tendency to climate warming with above-average temperatures and hours of sunshine is also making itself felt in the vineyard. The somewhat cooler high elevations are gaining increasingly in importance, since in the vineyards between 150 and 200 meters above sea level there is naturally more wind movement which can protect the grapes from moisture and thereby from fungal diseases and rotting. This positive ventilation allows the grapes to remain on the vine as long as possible, and at the same time promotes the ripening of healthy grapes.

LESS IS MORE

While "harvest as much as possible to fill the cellar and loft" was the maxim for centuries, quality winemaking today relies on reduction of output in order to produce quality instead of quantity, beginning in the vineyard itself. Decisive here is not so much the yield per hectare, but rather, per individual vine. With Riesling the average value, depending on soil structure, is between 1 and 2.5 liters of must per vine. In order to attain a useful yield reduction, that is, a balance between cost-effectiveness and quality, there are various options which depend on the climatic conditions of the region and on the location. Modern winemaking trims down the foliage before flowering begins, in order to reduce the potential energy supply to the leaves and thereby to allow fewer bunches to grow. This results in lower yields, and at the same time, through the ensuing loose berry formation, the risk of botrytis infestation decreases. The winemaker has a further option for yield reduction about four weeks after flowering in June. He or she can now thin out the crop and selectively cut out the resulting bunches. However, the so-called green harvest, which normally takes place in mid-August, has proved a failure with Riesling. Since nature seeks equilibrium, it shares out the available nutrients to the remaining grape bunches where a reduction of quantity has occurred. There then appear large juicy grapes, whose relatively thin skin can no longer take the strain. The grapes then squeeze each other and burst, and as a consequence are particularly liable to rotting.

GREENING THE VINEYARD

Whether vineyards should receive green cover depends on the location and on the water supply. If only a little water is available in relatively dry locations, then as a rule only every second row is covered with green vegetation. Moister soils, on the other hand, can accommodate greening of the entire area. A decisive factor for foliage treatment in the vineyard is the maximum assimilation with the best possible ventilation, which is individually dependent on the location of the vines. Since grapes can also suffer from sunburn, and thereby produce unwanted, bitter tannins in the grape skins, it is important to harden the grapes in good time against this risk. If namely the foliage is reduced early enough, the young grapes become accustomed to ultraviolet radiation and store up shielding agents in good time.

A MATTER OF TRAINING

The vine density and training system primarily depend on the location. Quality viticulture as a rule assumes about 4,000 vines per hectare, in some individual sites up to 10,000 Riesling vines are planted on one hectare. Vines are trained on wire trellises wherever mechanization is possible to any extent. Varying row-widths on the one hand suit the machines necessary for cultivation and harvesting, while on the other the vines should not take each other's light through too high or indeed too confined growth. Additionally, in this way an appropriate microclimate is ensured.

A healthy grape growth is a prerequisite for quality wine

RIESLING – GENUINE AND FEIGNED

Not every wine referred to as a Riesling is really a Riesling. Non-authentic representatives of this variety are Goldriesling, Cape Riesling, Welschriesling (Austria), the red wine variety Schwarzriesling (Pinot Meunier; Germany), Riesling Italico (Italy), Laski Rizling (former Yugoslavia), Emerald-Riesling, Missouri Riesling, Gray Riesling (USA), Olasz-Rizling (Hungary), Rizling Vlassky (Czech Republic) and Riesling de Banat (Romania).

RIESLING ON THE VINE

Single-vine training is used above all on extremely steep slopes – for instance on the Mosel, Saar and Ruwer, and on the Middle Rhine – in order to ensure sufficient sunlight for the vines. In such cases, the use of machines is either quite impossible or perhaps very restricted. Single-vine training requires above all cost-intensive manual labor. On the other hand it offers the winegrower on the steep sites the opportunity to move across the rows of vines, thus saving time and energy.

AUTUMNAL SELECTION

Despite all precautions taken by the wine grower and the availability of technical options for today's wine production, the vineyard continues to be a natural, and thus ultimately an unpredictable system with many risks. Particularly in the northerly cultivation of Riesling there is the constant risk of a sudden worsening of the weather in the form of frost, hail or cloudbursts. Accordingly, the grapes may develop differently in every season. If the winemakers intend to harvest the grapes suited to their wine type, then they must pick them selectively. This applies above all to the time-consuming selection of healthy grape bunches affected by botrytis, which is performed exclusively by hand in up to seven or eight pickings. If the grapes are damaged, a negative selection takes place, by which all the grapes that are not desired for the harvest are removed. Technology has also made progress in this area, and although modern harvesting machines cannot selectively pick, they can however be usefully employed in the harvest of healthy grapes without any negative effects on the harvested crop.

THE FIVE RIPENING STAGES IN THE LIFE OF A GRAPE

Unripe grapes

Unripe grapes yield immature and minor wines. If the still unripe grape skin becomes damaged by external influences, an early botrytis is formed and there is then the risk of the unwanted and negative sour rot.

Ripe grapes

As a rule, good levels of quality are achieved from ripe grapes. A potential occurrence of botrytis at this stage of ripening can be quite positive. Nevertheless, for fresh, dry Qualität and Kabinett wines the botrytis grapes must be carefully separated out during the harvest.

Fully ripe grapes

Fully ripe grapes are the prerequisite for wines with depth and structure and as a rule are the basic raw material for complex, dense wines, such as for instance "Erste und Grosse Gewächse" (see page 42). Particularly for these high quality grades, healthy grape material is a prerequisite, and a proportion of 5 to 10% of healthy botrytis is desired by many winemakers in order to give the wines more vigor and body. If the grapes are too severely affected by botrytis, then the grapes would be suited for the production of residual-sugar Spätlese wines, or – after selection – Auslese wines.

The ripeness of the grapes determines the quality and style of the wine

Overripe grapes

From overripe grapes emerge wines which, as a rule, and due to advanced botrytis, can no longer be made into dry wines. This crop forms the basis for Spätlese and Auslese wines with residual sugar and at the same time marks the crossover to the selected, botrytised sweet wines.

Dried grapes

Raisin-like, shriveled grapes, which as a rule occur only from mid-November onwards, are the result of the noble-rot botrytis. These grapes form the backbone of the botrytized Riesling-variants from Beerenauslese right up to Trockenbeerenauslese, for which several strict selection stages are necessary.

HEALTHY ROT – A CONTRADICTION?

Known for short as botrytis, this grape rot appears when the mold fungus *Botrytis cinerea* with its enzymes affects ripe and undamaged grapes and perforates their skins. Thus with

Shriveled grapes for botrytized wines

warmer and drier atmospheric conditions, over half of the water stored in the grapes can be lost through evaporation, and the sugar and aroma concentration increases. The fungus produces a number of chemical compounds, among others glycerol, gluconic acid and flavorings such as sotolon. This can go so far that a Trockenbeerenauslese is obtained whose must exhibits 2 to 2 1/2 times the sugar content of healthy grapes. Botrytis can occur during the entire vegetation phase of the vine, but it is desired only in the final ripening phase and

MEASURABLE QUALITY

How can one measure quality? By geographical provenance or by the must weight of the grape? In Germany and Austria the must weight is measured in degrees Oechsle. The degrees convey, through the amount of grape sugar, the ripeness of the grapes and hence the potential alcohol content. The Oechsle scale measures by how many grams per liter the specific gravity of the must exceeds that of water. If for example a liter of must weighs 1100 grams, then the must weight is 100 degrees Oechsle, since one liter of water weighs exactly 1000 grams.

Selective yield reduction is a precondition for the making of quality wines

for the majority of wine types it is not beneficial. Healthy botrytis, that is to say, botrytis desired by the winemaker, occurs above all in regions with a temperate climate that is ideally characterized by moist morning mists and sunny but cool fall days.

If the grapes are unable to dry off, particularly in warmer conditions and higher humidity, there is a danger that they will burst and that unwanted green mold will develop.

In invariably warm and above all dry climates, such as, for example in California, the botrytis fungus cannot even develop. The harvest of botrytis grapes usually requires a number of stages with experienced winepickers, during which only those grape bunches or individual grapes are picked which are in an optimal state of molding.

THE CELLAR – THE ADOPTED HOME

Defensive actionism is called for

That wines originate exclusively in the vineyard is only half the truth. The statement is aimed at the consumer, who presumes somehow that a natural product must be "pure", because wine ought not to be "made" but preferably "grow" and get into the bottle in the corresponding state. That's why in this context there is a preference – at least in the Old World – to speak not of the winemaker, but of the winegrower, vintner or cellarer. It is beyond dispute however, that even with the advantages of hi-tech wine cellars, high-class wines cannot be produced from bad grapes. Consequently, a high grape quality is required from the beginning, which should be detectable once again, later on, in the glass. In order to optimally express grape variety and terroir, the cellar machinery should preferably only support the processing of the grapes. Ideally, vineyard and cellar management complement one another and co-operate qualitatively, hand in hand.

TRENDSETTING

Generally binding rules do not exist. However, there are vinification concepts, which, like a cooking recipe, proceed in more or less standardized processing stages and guarantee reasonably high qualities. If however the winemaker intends to produce outstanding Rieslings, then healthy ambition, a desire for quality as well as unrestrained passion, and a

consistent weighing up of benefits and risk must complement the already available expertise. Each grape can be made into wine only once. What then happens, and with which intensity and in which direction in the cellar, is not only a decision of principle, but a continual challenge. The application of the cellar's technology must orient itself to the natural product, namely the grape, which is similar each year at best, but never identical. Most wine-growing estates produce their wines according to traditional methods, but more and more they are using the latest technology in order to exploit the quality potential of the grape even more sensitively and in a more explicit fashion. There are, depending on condition and degree of ripeness, various ways of pressing the juice out of the grapes.

THREE WAYS TO WINE

Whole-bunch pressing means that the grapes are put into the press directly after harvesting. This method is used above all to produce fruitily elegant Rieslings, which should be characterized by a finesse-rich, lightly exhilarating interplay between fruit and acidity. However, this pressing method usually leads to a lack of depth, substance, body and ability of the wine to age. This is because most flavorings are in the grape skins and they are not released during the relatively rapid pressing. Accordingly Rieslings, which should reflect their terroir, cannot exploit their full potential with this method. If unripe bunches are pressed whole, after a brief, youthful phase the wine tastes emaciated and thin. By means of whole-bunch pressing however, botrytis grapes and harvested overripe high-extract grapes can be processed into fruity Spätlese and Auslese wines, since the rapid pressing hinders the mold from getting into the must.

STANDARD

With the second – these days more common – method, the grapes are lightly squeezed by crushing before being pressed, so that the juice is released. This mechanical processing – before pressing – facilitates the release of the important ingredients from the grape skins, and thereby brings body and vigor, but also minerality and fruit into the wine.

MACERATION TIME

In order to impart more extract, complexity and aroma into Riesling wines, more and more frequently the actual pressing process is preceded by maceration. This involves letting the crushed grapes stand as a fruit mash for four to twelve hours in a recipient or in the press. During this period, significantly more aroma-specific ingredients pass from the grape skins into the must before it is pressed. The acidity can also be reduced in a natural way via a maceration time. The potassium released from the grape skins combines with the tartaric acid and forms tartrate crystals, which precipitate during fermentation. Tartrate is the crystal of potassium salts and therefore a hundred-per-cent natural product. The higher the temperature of the grapes, the faster the bio-chemical processes. Most winemakers prefer maceration times with temperatures between 10°C and a maximum of 18°C.

It is important that healthy and fully ripe grapes are used, since only then are the stalks woody. If, on the other hand, the stalks are still green, unwanted tannins are released, and a negative bitter taste appears in the wine.

FERMENTATION DOES IT

The discussion about what is good for a Riesling in its individual development phases or what runs contrary to its character depends on the climate and on the growth-influenced ripeness of the grapes, and this is something the winemaker is confronted with every year anew. The linchpin here is the acidity – the

The winemaker decides on the further processing of the grapes depending on their condition

significant mainstay of Riesling – and its opposite number, the fruit of the wine, in its various degrees of ripeness. The relation between these two, the style the winemaker intends to achieve – dry or with residual sugar – crucially depends on the fermentation process, since during alcoholic fermentation the sugar contained in the grapes is turned into alcohol.

SPONTANEOUS OR INFLUENCED?

Yeasts are catalysts which convert the must into wine and during the fermentation process cause new ingredients to arise. As to which yeasts should be used here – whether the naturally-occurring yeasts in the must or added, cultured yeasts – is a question much discussed today, and for some winemakers it is stylized into a shibboleth. While some insist on the natural – since these are said to produce longer living, more individual Rieslings which can demonstrate their complexity only after a certain ripening period – others say that Rieslings produced by fermentation using cultured yeasts demonstrate – above all in their youth – more clarity, more fruit and more complexity.

INDIVIDUAL RISK

As ever the truth is to be found somewhere in the middle. Firstly one should realize that 90% of wild yeasts are not at all suited for complete fermentation and can introduce undesirable flavor-forming features into the wine such as ethyl acetate (reminiscent of nail varnish remover), acetic acid and, smelling of bad eggs, hydrogen sulfide, a wine fault the Germans call böckser (goaty smell). This is a real risk that is increased when the grapes are not so healthy as they might be and thus additionally affected by micro-organisms. In

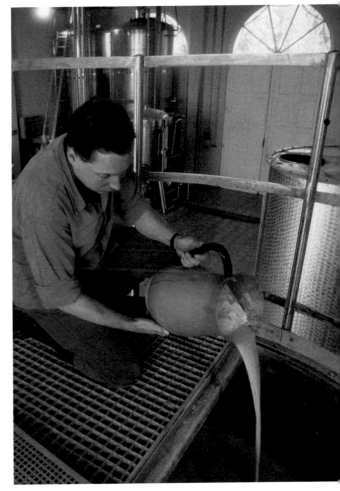

The addition of cultured yeasts allows a relatively unproblematic fermentation in the winemaker's desired style

order to minimize this risk, for over 100 years yeasts have been selected from successful spontaneous fermentations which, as cultured yeasts, can be introduced into the must. However, certain cultured yeasts can cause a banal, fruity uniformity in the wine, and in the opinion of the critics, it is precisely the individual natural yeasts that bring a certain amount of authentic terroir into the wine and thereby promote the individuality of Riesling.

Gleaming stainless-steel tanks are standard equipment even on many traditional estates

draws off many of the valuable aromas with it. The resulting wines tend to be one-dimensional and crude.

This problem appeared above all after the Second World War, as the stainless steel containers and concrete vats became ever larger and excess warmth could no longer be sufficiently released. The idea of cool fermentation was already developed in Germany in the 1950s, but only when it came to Europe from abroad in the early 90s, above all from the warmer cultivation regions, did the pendulum truly swing in this direction. Today, the standard fermentation temperature for Riesling lies between 15 and 18°C. In this temperature range the majority of aromas remain intact, and the varietal aroma of Riesling is not concealed by intrusive fruity fermentation aromas.

However, these are only guidelines. In reality, the fermentation temperature should be monitored daily, and depending on the progress, should be corrected with sure instinct. The decisive factor is that the yeasts are active at all. Fermentation should last at least four – and as a rule no longer than twelve – weeks. Too long a fermentation period involves the risk of the development of other microorganisms which at best would lead to a malolactic fermentation, and at worst would form volatile acids or cause the wine to oxidize.

A COOL HEAD IN A HOT PHASE

Temperature is an important instrument for controlling the speed of fermentation. An advantage is a rapid start, so that the must is protected from unwanted wild yeasts. If the fermentation then proceeds in an uncontrolled and turbulent fashion, much energy will be converted into warmth. The yeasts are further heated up, and the escaping carbonic acid

STAINLESS STEEL OR WOOD?

Gleaming stainless-steel tanks in a hi-tech cellar, or traditional wooden vats in romantic candlelight? The question of the right container for Riesling is in the first place dependent on the individual concepts of the winemakers themselves regarding the types of wine they would like to produce.

The decision to use stainless steel or wood initially has no influence on the quality of the wine. Rather, the selection of the container is a question of the desired wine style.

After wood had determined the processing of wine for centuries, in the last 30 years stainless steel has gradually moved into the cellar. What has long been standard in the food industry and in kitchens has also asserted itself in the wine industry. Stainless steel permits impeccable hygiene, can be cleaned without any problem, is absolutely neutral to the taste, and has only little effect on the product which is processed or stored in it. Since stainless steel containers are absolutely airtight, the wine – when the tank is completely full – does not come into contact with oxygen. This reductive processing of Rieslings in stainless steel is suitable above all for lacy, finesse-rich and light wines that live by their markedly fresh fruitiness.

Reductive processing is usually combined with cool fermentation and since the 1980s has been considered worldwide as standard for the production of white wines. Even in the cellars of old wine estates steeped in tradition, this method has caused a veritable boom in stainless steel. With the trend towards reductive processing, there is also the implication of a certain uniformity of Rieslings. This is due however, more to cool fermentation and to the concurrently propagated rapid processing of the grapes, which allows no time for extraction of the grapes' own ingredients.

BACK TO WOOD

Nowadays, Riesling processing in wooden vats is gaining in importance once again, especially in the younger generation. Some winemakers rely on a combination of options: the must is fermented in a steel tank, and the young wine matures in a wooden vat or barrel. Nevertheless, in traditional cellars with wooden vats we must distinguish between those made of seasoned wood and those made of new oak.

In the case of the seasoned vats, the wood is virtually neutral and scarcely imparts any taste to the wine, in contrast to new "barrique" barrels. The dominant aroma from these barrels made of new oak is desired rather for acidity-poor and alcohol-rich white wines, so as to give the alcohol – for want of acidity – a sensory counterpart. With Riesling, which brings with it a vigorous, natural acidity, processing in 225-liter barrique barrels can be rather counterproductive and has therefore not prevailed.

On the other hand with Riesling, the traditional, large wooden vat is coming back into fashion, because the fine pores of natural wood allow a certain amount of oxygen into the wine and thereby speed up its clarification, stabilization and maturing. Some winemakers are convinced that this can positively influence the development of full-bodied, complex and luxuriant Rieslings and contribute to the unfolding of aromas. Other winemakers on the other hand attempt, particularly via reductive processing, to "slim down" these massive Rieslings.

LOCATION, LOCATION, LOCATION

Since wood – in contrast to stainless steel – is an active natural material and interacts with its

Traditional wooden vats are experiencing a comeback particularly among the younger generation of winemakers

surroundings, a certain importance attaches to the location of the barrels. In cool, damp cellars, only a relatively small exchange of oxygen takes place through the pores in the wood – a process that benefits lacier, fruitier wines.

In contrast, the pores open at higher cellar temperatures and speed up the oxidation pro-cess, which can be an advantage principally for red wines. As a natural product, wooden barrels also need more care and maintenance, and with careless cellar management can be the cause of fusty traces and sources of infec-tion from unwanted lactic acid bacteria or *brettanomyces,* which can produce a hint of medicine or sweat.

THE THRILL OF ACIDITY

Riesling has acidity! Within this pithy but undeniable statement, the entire problem is summed up: Riesling is unique and unmistakable, but for some people also inaccessible. Its natural and distinct acidity appears to be a problem in itself for a certain segment of the public taste, because this inherent characteristic comes across itself, as with no other grape variety, from piquant to distinctly formed and provokes dissent. The acidity thereby forms the soul and the backbone of Riesling and gives it a refreshing flavor. Ultimately, Rieslings, above all those from relatively cool regions, must owe to this acidity their lacy taste, the brilliance and especially the tension between the acidity and the fruity sweetness – like a juicy, crisp apple which has grown in a cool climate zone and whose stimulating effect and delicate flavor create a desire for the next bite.

A DELICATE BALANCING ACT

The decisive question is however how much acidity a Riesling must have in order to maintain its character, while not placing it in the acid category. And how high must the acidity be above all in the case of botrytized and residual-sugar Rieslings, in order to balance the sweetness with a contrasting partner, a balance which ultimately constitutes the finesse-rich, Riesling-typical interplay. There is no silver-bullet solution linked conclusively to analysis data. The taste balance of the individual parameters must be right. Whether, in the end, a Riesling reveals too high a level of acidity is basically not a question of analytics. In such a case, one's own tastebuds are the exclusive decision-maker, since appraisal of the acid is a matter of sensory balance:

residual-sugar wines require by way of compensation a more vigorous acidity, so that the sweetness is not too ponderous, but retains its subtle, elegant playfulness. Rieslings in the dry range, where the residual sweetness is limited, evince as a rule accordingly low acidity values. If the acidity here is too high, it becomes the sole defining sensory factor, and the wine will simply taste sour.

DON'T BE AFRAID OF ACIDITY

"One of the great differences between Riesling and other wines is the acidity. Even for the human stomach acidity is not unusual, it itself produces hydrochloric acid. This acid helps the stomach to prepare food for absorption into the bloodstream. After passage of the food through the stomach there then occurs further digestion in the duodenum. Here, the pancreas adds its digestive juices. One of the tasks of the pancreas is to neutralize the gastric acid, so that it can be assimilated by the mucous membranes without problem. The acidity contributed by the Riesling is neutralized in the same way and finally assimilated. When drunk in normal doses, usually up to half a liter for example when eating, then in a healthy person there is no problem with the Riesling's acidity. On the contrary: it assists digestion. Only after clearly excessive wine consumption can acidosis occur. Here as elsewhere the rule is: always drink at least the same amount of water as wine."

Dr. Rainer Terhedebrügge MD

NOTHING DOING WITHOUT ACID

The most important organic acids are tartaric acid and – in somewhat lower concentration – malic acid. The less mature a wine is, the higher the proportion of malic acid. In addition there are small amounts of lactic acid, citric acid, succinic acid, acetic acid, and carbonic acid. With botrytized Rieslings a white salt on the underside of the cork betrays the presence of gluconic acid formed by the botrytis fungus. In principle acids restrain the growth of harmful bacteria and keep the wine micro-biologically stable.

CASTRATED RIESLING?

That the discussion pro or contra Riesling starts with acidity is perhaps understandable, but immediately confronts the variety with its essential character attributes. Starting during the ripening process, a natural acidity reduction takes place in the grapes. With a maceration period, acidity is also reduced, and there exists the possibility of chemical de-acidification. However, the common and internationally proven method is malolactic fermentation. Here, lactic acid bacteria transform malic acid, existing naturally in wine, into milder lactic acid while releasing carbon dioxide. Riesling wines can thereby become softer, creamier and rounder. Usually the winemaker subjects only a part of his or her Riesling batch to the process of malolactic fermentation and blends it later with the untreated portion. The debate on whether Riesling should align itself to an assumed international taste through the reduction of its acidity is cur-

rently raging in the classic Riesling regions. For the reduction of acidity also leads to a change in the flavor and in the intensity of fruit. Above all, the citrus and peach aromas typical of Riesling can be reduced or can completely disappear during malolactic fermentation. If malolactic fermentation is interrupted before transformation of the malic acid is complete, an unpleasant lactic acid tinge can occur, reminiscent of yoghurt, whey, cheese and in extreme cases even of sauerkraut.

SENSITIVITY TO NATURE

Organic viticulture and Riesling

Ecology is an increasingly important aspect of a healthy environment and diet. This is also true of wine, especially of Riesling, which is mainly cultivated by small and middle-sized businesses and thereby – in contrast to industrial mass production – leaves enough leeway for organic production methods.

When there is talk these days of organic methods in wine production, then it is of near-natural wine cultivation in which all measures are considered which, viewed holistically, show consideration for nature. What was ridiculed just a few years ago, is now part of the standard program of many prestigious winemakers in all winegrowing regions. Conventional and organic winemaking have come closer together, and compromises have been made on both sides in order to give precedence to nature. The idea of organic wine production gained in popularity in the 1980s as traces of pesticides were found in foods and the fear of poisonous substances inevitably extended to wine.

It is difficult to draw an exact line between conventional and organic viticulture. More and more conventional businesses are doing without herbicides and reducing the application of nitrogenous fertilizers. Indeed, in the monoculture of wine production the winemaker is economically dependent upon the soil and the vines rooted in it, and the question is, how this delicate natural system can be protected, in the long term and sustainably, in order to make the vines lastingly more resistant. If technological options in the cellars, through long experience, appear to be largely optimized, then above all the cultivation measures in the vineyard must now be gradually improved in order to establish and to stabilize a healthy and environmentally compatible system.

UNITY IN VARIATION

There are varying opinions as to the detailed definition of organic winemaking. Agreement exists about not introducing substances into the soil that do not directly originate from natural sources. Thus the soil system should be healthily maintained as the most important resource for the vine and the winemakers' families without chemical resources or synthetic sprays and mineral fertilizers. Organic winegrowers therefore rely on the deliberate reproduction of the natural enemies of the pests, in order to reduce their influence. Accordingly, organic viticulture is increasingly adopting a preventive approach, which at the same time is more labor-intensive.

Furthermore, organic wine production aspires to the protection of the environment through prevention of soil erosion and pollution. The intention is, in all aspects of wine production, to find the natural method in order to promote the biological diversity of the ecosystem and thereby to diminish somewhat

A largely unspoiled natural environment is an essential requirement for organic wine making

the monocultural character of wine production. This requires, amongst other things, the targeted planting of green manure, which plays an important role in the establishment of beneficial organisms, which make a significant contribution to the biological balance and which in turn eliminate pests such as the spider mite in a natural way. Organic winegrowers use exclusively biological fertilizers, for example in the form of decomposed plant material such as straw and compost, or animal manure.

BIODYNAMIC WINE PRODUCTION

This method of alternative wine production is essentially based on the theories of the Austrian nature-philosopher Rudolf Steiner (1861–1925). Biodynamic wine production is concerned with the health of the soil and a natural equilibrium. In the production process, other aspects such as the phases of the moon, the sun's cycles, the stars and the influence of the cosmos are included. Through this alignment to the natural rhythm of nature, healthier plants are ultimately deemed to grow. And thus, just as the ebb and flow of the tides are dependent upon the gravitational pull of the moon, so also according to biodynamics the sprouting and the growth of plants should respond to phases of the moon. Biodynamics relies above all on the self-healing powers of nature and on homoeopathy in the vineyard.

The three most important substances for biodynamic wine are: cow dung for the soil, horn dung for the roots, and cow horns, filled with silica dust and buried in the soil to enhance the photosynthesis of the foliage.

PRO AND CONTRA

All the methods have advantages and disadvantages, there is no blanket correct or wrong way. On the contrary, the Riesling maker must adjust his method individually to the prevailing natural and economic conditions. Thus usually the happy medium promises the best solution. The healthy maintenance of the soil can be taken into consideration while at the same time minimizing the risks of pest damage to the ripe grapes that result particularly from Riesling's long vegetation phases.

WITH THANKS TO ECOLOGY

In the case of wine, organic quality – in contrast to organic meat as opposed to meat from factory farming, or organic tomatoes as opposed to those grown on cotton wool with nutrient fluids – cannot, or can only seldom, be tasted or smelt. However, organic winemakers have proved in the last few years that

top wines can certainly be produced on their soils, wines distinguished by considerable mineral presence and their terroir. It has been scientifically proved that organic growing allows vines to put down deeper roots and thus nourish themselves better. Considering all the natural difficulties with which organic winemaking is associated, it is to its credit to have once again awoken a sensibility in many winemakers for the natural system of the vineyard.

The Alsatian winemaker Jean-Michel Deiss is a committed advocate of biodynamic winemaking and terroir wines

CHAPTER 2

THE WORLD OF RIESLING

DIVERSITY
ALL AROUND THE GLOBE

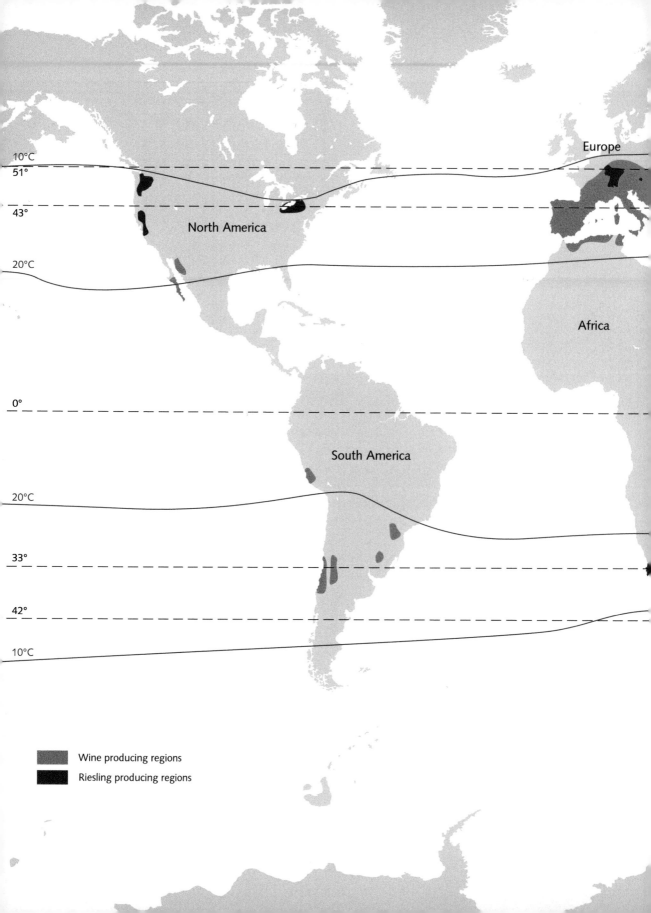

10°C
51°
43°
20°C

Europe

North America

Africa

0°

South America

20°C
33°
42°
10°C

Wine producing regions
Riesling producing regions

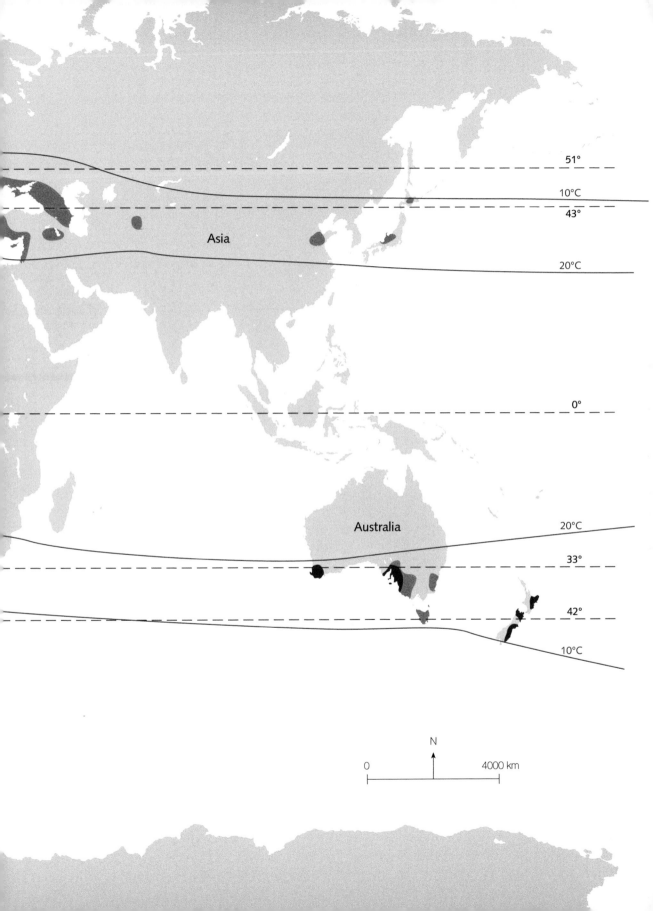

51°

10°C

43°

Asia

20°C

0°

Australia

20°C

33°

42°

10°C

N

0   4000 km

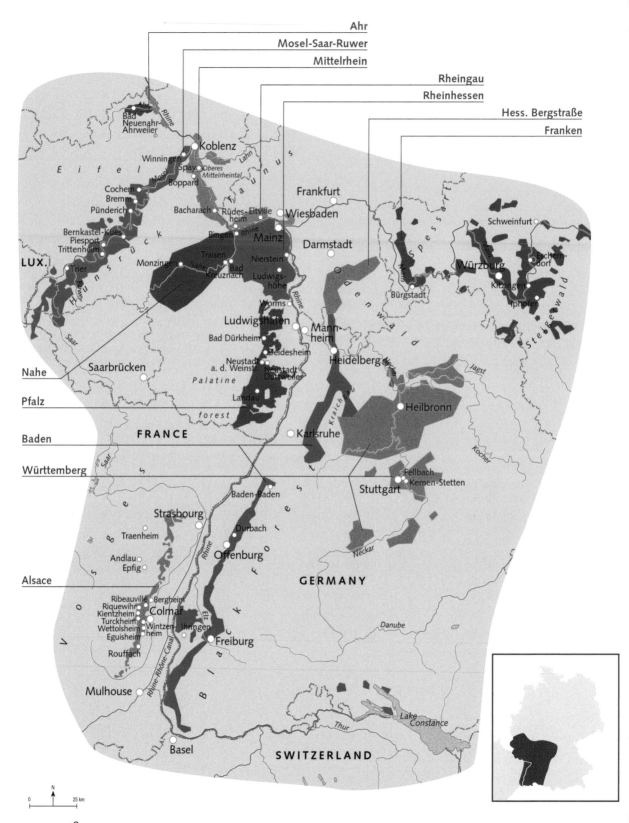

Ahr

Mosel-Saar-Ruwer

Mittelrhein

Rheingau

Rheinhessen

Hess. Bergstraße

Franken

Ahr

Bad
Neuenahr-
Ahrweiler

Koblenz

Eifel

Winningen
Spay
Boppard

*Oberes
Mittelrheintal*

Lahn

Rhine

Taunus

Frankfurt

Spessart

Schweinfurt

Cochem
Bremm

Pünderich

Bacharach
Rüdes- Eltville
heim

Bingen   *Rhine*

Wiesbaden

Mainz

Darmstadt

Würzburg

Main

Escherns-
dorf

Mosel

Bernkastel-Kues
Piesport
Trittenheim

Trier

Hunsrück

Traisen

Monzingen   *Nahe*

Nierstein

Ludwigs-
höhe

Rhine

Kitzingen

Iphofen

Steigerwald

Bad
Kreuznach

Ruwer

Saar

LUX.

Worms

Odenwald

Bürgstadt

Ludwigshafen

Mann-
heim

Neckar

Jagst

Nahe

Saarbrücken

Bad Dürkheim

Palatine

Deidesheim

Neustadt
a. d. Weinstr. Neustadt
Dürrweiler

Heidelberg

Kraichgau

Heilbronn

Kocher

Pfalz

Landau

forest

Baden

FRANCE

Karlsruhe

Württemberg

Saar

Neckar

Fellbach
Kernen-Stetten

Stuttgart

Baden-Baden

Vosges

Strasbourg

Traenheim

Durbach

Offenburg

Andlau
Epfig

B l a c k   F o r e s t

GERMANY

Alsace

Ribeauvillé Bergheim
Riquewihr
Kientzheim
Turckheim
Wettolsheim
Eguisheim

Colmar

Wintzen- Ihringen
heim

Freiburg

Elz

Danube

Rouffach

Rhine-Rhône-Canal

Mulhouse

Thur

Lake
Constance

Basel

SWITZERLAND

N

0   25 km

GERMANY

The home of Riesling

Riesling cultivation-zone latitudes:
48° to 51° N.
Total vine area: 102,240 hectares
Riesling: 20,627 hectares, represents
20.2% of all German vineyards,
61.4% worldwide
Main risks for viticulture: frost
Average temperature in July: 19°C

Some of the best Rieslings grow on German soil, this is indisputable, and there were always excellent German Riesling wines, even in times when the grape variety was not in vogue. Indeed, with regard to its acceptance, German Riesling has time and again striven through deep vales of tears and had to serve for all sorts of flavor experiments: from bone dry to sugary-sweet and back again. The sour or sweet wines exhibited acidity values which either brought all taste nerves to the fore in a flash, or degraded Riesling into a dull, weary wine. The oenological pendulum swung from one extreme to the other.

MOST FAVORABLE CONDITIONS

That the Germans made it so difficult for their Riesling is actually baffling, since the varied range of soils in the growing areas is the reliable guarantor for the flavor diversity and the fascination of German Rieslings. And this is in spite of – or precisely because of – the fact that Germany is a marginal zone for wine-growing. The classic Riesling regions lie near the 51st parallel, which represents the northernmost climatic boundary for vine cultivation. A stroke of luck for Riesling: the little round grape prefers cooler zones, and these are to be found above all in the growing areas of northern Germany. Influenced by a continental climate – warm summer and cold winter – Riesling ripens here only slowly and as a rule is picked only from mid-October to the end of November. The consequence of this long ripening period is a flavor diversity ranging from simple Qualitätswein to botrytized specialties and delicate ice wines.

LOSS AND GAIN OF IMAGE

In the 19th century, Riesling was one of the classic quartet of top-class wines: Bordeaux red, Burgundian white and red, and Riesling from the Rhine and Mosel. However, while the French continually improved their position, Riesling slowly but surely bowed out of this constellation. Its peaks and troughs had various reasons. The first signs already became apparent after World War I in 1918, as the lucrative market of the entire European aristocracy had broken down almost overnight and thereby also the marketing instrument of "purveyors by royal appointment" disappeared. In addition there was the severe economic situation itself in the countries that previously imported German wines. After World War II as well, trade was at rock bottom. Many old sales markets were closed to German wines.

PRODUCTION EUPHORIA

In the mid-1950s, as the euphoria of the German economic miracle began to take effect, the old idea of agriculture – to produce as much as possible – with assistance from advancing technological applications, in wine-making as well, experienced a completely new production dimension. At the same time, science applied itself intensively to the cultivation of high-yielding new varieties. In this way the old craft production methods successively disappeared into obscurity, and human manpower was deliberately replaced by increasing automation and advancing technology.

WINEGROWER OR WINEMAKER?

Winegrowers could now become active wine-makers, with the possibility of systematic control of fermentation, which until now they had to leave to nature and to the vagaries of the fermentation yeasts, but from now on could actively define the wine style. Now, wine was being produced at ever more economical prices which the market was prepared to absorb. And after years of privation, these were above all sweet and cheap wines, which had only the attribute "süss" (sweet) in common with the tradition of great botrytized Rieslings or elegant, finesse-rich residual-sweet Riesling Spätlese wines. It was a baleful development: from then on "süss" was considered as a synonym for cheap, simple, German.

A DIFFICULT RELATIONSHIP

The former high regard for German Riesling not only received profound dents to its image

in its homeland, Riesling became once again what it actually is: an outsider, this time how- ever not a highly-regarded outsider, but an ignored one, without the allure of its variety and without the luster of its complexity. This development was also supported by a desire for gustatory discovery and joy for gustatory experimentation on the part of the post-war generation and, going hand-in-hand with this, an open rejection of German tradition, to which also Riesling belonged. The dusty im- age of a long-outdated romance of wine no longer had a place in a new, cosmopolitan and tolerant society. Germany then consequently became one of the world's biggest import markets for foreign wines, and they had little competition. While 1976 was still a peak year for Riesling, there followed thereafter rainy, weak vintages of mediocre quality.

In addition, there was the fact that the market for sickly-sweet wine had grown weary, because it was so one-sided and not really suited to accompanying food. A style-change to dry white wines and to improved quality was inevitable. However, it still took until the early 1990s for Riesling to once again serious- ly establish itself – above all in top-class gas- tronomy.

REGULATIONS FOR WINES

Even the German parliament succeeded in ac- celebrating the loss of image of German wine with the new wine law of 1971. The idea of creating ascending Prädikat designations defined solely by increasing sugar concen- trations in the grapes when they are picked could ultimately not guarantee quality. The

reorganization of the old vineyard sites (Lagen) and the accompanying establishment of new "Grosslagen" (literally, "large sites", a wine-law designation for a group of individ- ual vineyards which can cover quite a large area) and the invention of fantasy names, now allowed very ordinary wines to parade under the label of famous wine locations. The result was a flood of new designations that simply overburdened the majority of customers – above all in the export market. To this day, the German wine industry continues to ignore this fact. It is constantly creating new terms and designations, without at the same time making a clean break with old ways.

AWAKENING OF NEW QUALITY CONCEPTS

At the end of the 1980s, there was a noticeable awakening in terms of quality which has con- tinued to this day and which has produced first-class Rieslings in the last few years. Ger- many experienced a renaissance in its Quali- tätswein and Riesling was rediscovered by a new generation of winemakers. This new popularity arose thanks to winegrowers who thought and acted in logically consistent fash- ion, to improved training, to dedicated deal- ers, to open-minded restaurateurs, and not least also to an interested press, which made Riesling a subject of public discussion.

German Riesling also enjoyed increasing popularity abroad and the demand rose. Ries- ling fits into our times; it offers a variety in taste with comparatively low alcohol levels. Certainly, the increasing interest in foreign cultures and cooking has contributed to this change. Particularly for Asian specialties that distinguish themselves in some cases through particularly intensive aromas, Riesling is an outstanding companion.

The botrytized Rieslings from the Scharzhofberger estate are legendary and well known around the world

CLASSIFICATION

The emphasizing of particular vineyards has a tradition in all the important wine-producing regions of the world. Even since ancient times, man has attempted to divide wine into quality categories and thereby to classify them. The simplest, but particularly effective grading was by price, a recognizable regulator for qualitative differentiation. The monastic wine-world of Europe in the 12th century took up this classification and combined it with the term "cabinet": especially high-quality wines that were stored in a corresponding "cabinet cellar" were thus designated. From 1498, "crescentia" appeared for the first time in the cellar inventories of Eberbach Monastery in the Rheingau as "growths from especial sites". The quality expressions of Spätlese and Auslese were used for the first time in Germany only in the 18th century, after the quality of the late and selective harvest was recognized and systematized.

THE CENTURY OF CLASSIFICATIONS

In the 19th century the world of wine stepped into the century of classifications. In 1855, by order of Napoleon III, the most important châteaux of the Bordelais were classified by the Bordeaux chamber of commerce for the World Exhibition in Paris: the Grands Crus Classés of Médoc. At the same time the Sauternes and Barsac zones were graded. After 1866, following the Austro-Prussian War, in the districts newly acquired by Prussia in Germany, winegrowing maps served as the basis for classification of vineyard sites. The Rheingau made a start with this in 1885. The Dahlen map was based on the quality of the soil, and the land tax entries of the vineyards associated with it. This classification endured into the 1920s, but since then this distinguishing element of site classification fell somewhat into oblivion.

THE GERMAN WINE LAW

With the German wine law of 1971 a new classification was created, which linked the quality grades and Prädikat distinctions to the must weights at the time of picking. The unit of measurement, the "degree Oechsle" defines whether the must may later be offered as Qualitätswein or as Kabinett, Spätlese, Auslese, Beerenauslese, or Trockenbeerenauslese. The minimum Oechsle degrees vary from region to region; a Kabinett from the Mosel is allowed to have a lower must weight than the same Prädikat from Baden. In the years from 1987 onward, the Charta Association of the Rheingau, which was founded in 1984, once again took up the tradition of the Dahlen map of 1885, and classified the vineyards of its members. In the following years, parallel classification initiatives developed in the Pfalz, in Rheinhessen and along the Nahe river.

ERSTE GEWÄCHSE AND GROSSE GEWÄCHSE

This idea initially witnessed its official legitimization in the Rheingau, where wines from officially classified sites have been allowed to be described as "Erste Lage" (prime site) since the 1999 vintage. On this basis, the combined producers in the Verband deutscher Prädikatsweingüter (VDP) – association of German Prädikat wine estates) decided in 2002 on a system of classification for the "Grosses Gewächs" (grand cru). This involves primarily dry Riesling wines from the best sites. However, particularly in the southern growing areas, other traditional grape varieties are also taken into account. Quite confusing is the fact that the individual regional associations of the VDP have until now fixed very varying criteria as a basis both for the designation of the quality grade and for the maximum level of residual sugar. Still not decided is whether, for the designation "Grosses Gewächs," legal recognition is sought after or whether it should remain a private voluntary arrangement between members of the VDP.

The designation "Erste Lage" (prime site) denotes on the other hand, not primarily a dry wine type, but differentiates simply between first-class and ordinary vineyard sites from which wines of varying quality grades and flavors can originate. Nevertheless, a dry "Grosses Gewächs" must, if it is indeed the best wine of a particular winery, logically have grown in the "Erste Lage". The discussion of how far this classification should go, and which exact limitations for all members of the VDP should be binding, has up to now not been brought to a conclusion, owing to the varying points of view in the German growing areas.

LEGAL CLASSIFICATION OF GERMAN WINES

The following quality classes and quality grades are distinguished and, accordingly, every German wine must be declared with one of these designations:

Tafelwein

German table wine must exclusively originate from German-harvested grapes from authorized vine areas and grape varieties. In Germany, in comparison with other wine-producing countries, only small quantities of Tafelwein are produced. Chaptalization is allowed for the purpose of increasing alcohol content.

Landwein

German Landwein is an elevated grade of Tafelwein. With Landwein, also the area from which the grapes originate must be declared on the label. Landwein is always dry or medium-dry and chaptalization is allowed.

Qualitätswein bestimmter Anbaugebiete (Q.b.A)

This is the largest group of German wines. Qualitätswein must originate entirely from one of the 13 German growing areas. For every Qualitätswein, according to the grape variety and growing area, minimum values for natural alcohol content are specified. Qualitätswein, like Tafelwein and Landwein, is allowed to be chaptalized.

Qualitätswein mit Prädikat (Q.m.P)

This is an officially monitored wine of higher quality that may not be chaptalized. The prescribed minimum must weights vary, according to designation, grape variety and growing area.

Kabinett: a designation for fine, lighter wines from ripe grapes with relatively low alcohol level.

Spätlese: a designation for wines from fully-ripe grapes. The picking may take place at the earliest seven days after the beginning of the general harvest.

Auslese: a designation for high-value wines from particularly ripe grapes, which can be developed into dry as well as residual-sugar wines.

Beerenauslese: a designation for botrytized wines from overripe, noble-rot, botrytis-affected grapes with a high residual-sugar content. The grapes are individually selected by hand.

Trockenbeerenauslese: a designation for bot-ryized wines that are produced from raisin-like shriveled hand-selected grapes. The grapes are even more selectively picked.

Eiswein (ice wine): a designation for wines from grapes that are pressed in a frozen state, at least -7°C, and from which then only the fruit concentrate can be pressed out. The quality of the grapes must conform to those of a Beerenauslese.

ERSTES GEWÄCHS RHEINGAU

A good third of the vine growing areas of the Rheingau are specified as classified sites, which may be planted exclusively with Riesling or Spätburgunder (Pinot Noir). The site map takes not only quality-continuity of the vineyard into account, but also climatic and soil conditions. A further criterion is strict selection; a maximum of 50 hectoliters per hectare. Selective picking by hand is obligatory, along with the monitoring of color, smell and taste.

Residual sugar content may not exceed 13 grams per liter. All "Erste Gewächse" display on the label the three Romanesque arches on a black band. The wines may only be offered for sale from September 1 of the year following the harvest.

GROSSES GEWÄCHS VDP

The VDP demands similar criteria for the classification of the dry "Grosse Gewächse". Accordingly, the wines must originate from classified sites, with narrow, set limits, in which it can be verified that wines with a sustained, high degree of ripeness have been produced over a long period of time. The "Grosse Gewächse" must be produced exclusively from regionally specified grape varieties in Spätlese quality using traditional production methods. The crop is here also limited to 50 hectoliters per hectare. The wines may only be marketed from September 1 of the year following the harvest, red varieties in fact not until the second year after the harvest. VDP-businesses that produce Grosse Gewächse therefore dispense with the designation "Auslese trocken" for wines from identical sites and grape varieties.

CLASSIC AND SELECTION

In the year 2000, under the direction of the German wine institute, two new denominations were introduced: "Classic" and "Selection" (these are the original spellings). The term "Classic" includes vintage wines from classic regionally-typical grape varieties with a full-bodied, powerful and aromatic flavor profile. The residual-sugar content of the wine may be twice as high as its acid content, but no more than 15 grams. "Classic" wines may not be labeled with the name of either the commune or the vineyard. The intention is for them to reflect a wine of the category "grand ordinaire" in the sense of dry to off-dry. Under the term "Selection", vintage wines of particular quality are offered from delimited individual low yield vineyards – maximum 60 hectoliters per hectare – from which the grapes have been hand picked. The wines must be dry, with less than nine grams of residual sugar per liter. Only on the case of a Riesling with an accent of acidity are up to twelve grams allowed. Selection wines may be sold no earlier than a year after harvesting – at the earliest however on September 1 of the year following the harvest.

VIEWS AND OPINIONS ON CLASSIFICATION

Top German wines

"We are only at the beginning of a classification and it is a cultural task of generations, to which there cannot be given any quick, serious answer. Wine cultivation has for too long been conducted as legally-defined arable farming and only slowly are we once again moving closer to the wonder of wine from the point of view of the location, or let us say terroir. The profile of the best German wines must be clearly defined at the top, and above all must reflect their place of birth. This is possible only via strictly allotted site concepts and not via wine concepts. Therefore, we must attempt to bring the wines, which should shine, into unison with site names, flavor images, nature and brand. We require an individual answer to the general question: 'What do I get when I buy a bottle of first-class German wine?'"

Michael Prinz zu Salm-Salm,
President of the VDP

Open site-classification

"In Germany, we need a general designation for dry premium wines. It is undisputed that first-class quality has to do with the vineyard, the vintage and the work of the winemaker. Predestined locations can be clearly defined and delimited by one of a number of factors. Alongside this and according to the vintage, there must remain tolerance within a generously delimited winegrowing area and each individual wine must be tested for its outstanding quality. In principle, such a classification system must be open to all wine-growers, insofar as they own vineyards with-in the corresponding delimitation. Restric-tions concerning the varieties or the wine style, or whether particular designations such as grape variety or site names should only be used for classified wines of origin, can be defined in businesses, groupings or regions. Those actually affected should be the ones responsible for the classification, its designations, implementation and enforcement."

Armin Göring, Director of the
German Wine Institute, Mainz

Hope for German wine

"Firstly, it is important to differentiate between the classification of a wine estate in the Bordelaise sense and that of a vineyard as in Burgundy. In the absence of objective criteria and for reasons of constitutional law, an official estate classification is out of the question in Germany. In contrast, that a site classification is possible is proved by the sharply delimited parcels of land of the Rheingau sites, in which, among others, the 'dry Erstes Gewächs' is produced. However, as mentioned, other wine types too. To a large extent it is a matter of emphasizing a good site, that is to say, a site classification. The Grosses Gewächs of the VDP follows the same principle: it is a dry first-class wine from an 'Erste Lage' (prime site), from which also fruity and botrytized wines originate and where – above all in the southern regions – other traditional varieties other than Riesling can flourish. There is therefore hope for German wine, but it will however remain complicated in the future too!"

Armin Diel, wine critic and VDP
chairman in the Nahe region

Rows of vines planted on steep slopes make work difficult in the vineyards along the Mosel

MOSEL-SAAR-RUWER

Total vine area: 9,266 hectares
Riesling: 5,294 hectares,
represents 57.1% of the vine areas in
the region, 17.5% of all German vine areas,
15.7% worldwide

Sub-divided into Mosel, Saar and Ruwer, the wine growing region taken as a whole consists not only of a much loved cultural landscape, but is also one of the most fascinating wine-growing areas in the world. Where wine-growers cultivate steep sites and terrace viti-culture on stony inclines of the narrow river valleys at dizzy heights, enthusiasm and passion play a very important role. Without elaborate manual labor here, there is never any progress; in some places even cable winches cannot be installed. In order to manage one hectare of vines on the Mosel, around 1,200 working hours must be spent. In the Pfalz, success is possible with much less than half that amount.

TRENDSETTING

The region significantly represents a wine style which, when perfected, produces mag-nificent, delicate Kabinett wines and fruity, finesse-rich Spätlese wines with beguiling minerality and fine acidity interplay. Further-more, the Mosel is one of the famous German growing areas with a great tradition of botry-tized Rieslings. They have a good capacity for aging and even after decades evince astound-ing freshness and a dance-like character. In the sheltered river valleys, Riesling finds the ideal conditions for a long ripening period, on warmth-retaining slate soils. As a rule, the grape harvest lasts until long into November, and sometimes even into December.

THE DARK SIDE

In the 1970s, along with the growing areas in the tributary valleys, winegrowing was ex-tended into the plains along the Mosel that are only moderately suited to viticulture. With the production of cheap, easy-drinking wines, the great name that Mosel wine once had at home and abroad was gradually demolished. The "spirits of the cellar" that had been called forth became a burden, the wine once famous for its subtleties developed into "sugar-water", and at the same time prices hit rock bottom.

GLIMMERS OF LIGHT

Nevertheless, in the second half of the last century there were some bastions of Riesling culture which held up the reputation of the Mosel region. Wine estates such as Egon Müller, Maximin Grünhaus, Joh. Jos. Prüm and Fritz Haag have never participated in fashionable trends and for decades they have played a solid role with their Riesling wines in the world wine league. Alongside these classic players in the region's top class, who in the last few years have been joined by the likes of Reinhold Haart, Ernst Loosen, Johannes Selbach and Christoph Tyrell, there are also young upward-climbers such as Thomas Haag, Markus Molitor, Clemens Busch, Nik Weis and Eva Clüsserath. All these names prove that one does not have to worry greatly about the future of the Mosel. Emphasizing interesting features recently are winemakers in the same mold as Reinhard Löwenstein or Roman Niewodniczanski. They rely more on voluminous, creamier Riesling wines with suppleness and opulence, and less on the elegant, playful lightness of the classic line.

RHEINGAU

Total vine area: 3,137 hectares
Riesling: 2,452 hectares, represents 78.2% of the vine areas in the region, 8.1% of all German vine areas, 7.3% worldwide

The Rheingau is associated with Riesling like no other region in the world. On around 3,200 hectares of vineyard area, this little region has today the worldwide highest Riesling proportion of almost 80% and thus a very clear Riesling profile. In the vineyards facing south and southwest one finds gravel, sand and loamy to clay soils, interspersed with marl and loess. The lower Rheingau at Rüdesheim and the high sites at Kiedrich and Rauenthal are characterized by quartzite as well as weathered slate soils. With deep forests, the Rheingau hills provide adequate protection from the raw north winds.

THE CRADLE OF WINE CULTURE

Wine history has been written in the Rheingau since the Middle Ages. The former Benedictine monastery of Johannisberg – now Schloss Johannisberg – and the Cistercian abbey of Eberbach – now the state wine estates of Eberbach monastery – are believed to be the birthplace of quality terms such as Kabinett, Spätlese and Auslese. Other aristocratic estates such as Schloss Vollrads, Schloss Schönborn, Schloss Reinhartshausen or Freiherr Langwerth von Simmern look back in just the same way upon a glorious past.

HARD TIMES

From the mid-1980s, the Rheingau experienced a bitter, sharp decline accompanied by successive bad vintages. In addition to the weakness of the region the neighboring regions of the Pfalz, Nahe and Rheinhessen, were catching up, focussing more and more on quality. World-famous wine estates suddenly found themselves in the German mid-range category, and operations rich in tradition such as Schloss Eltz and Schloss Groenesteyn completely disappeared from the scene. Not until the arrival of a new generation of winegrowers who were all from family businesses, for instance Bernhard Breuer, Wilhelm Weil, Gunter Künstler and Peter Jakob Kühn, with an uncompromising quality offensive, was a Rheingau Riesling renaissance made possible. They were followed by young talents such as Johannes Eser, Johannes Leitz, Andreas Spreitzer and Reiner Flick, who are today among the established top elements of the region.

FORERUNNERS IN CLASSIFICATION

The emphasizing of distinctly noteworthy vineyards has a tradition in the Rheingau. It stretches from the Cistercian monks via Thomas Jefferson (1788) up to Goethe, who in his 1814 Rheingau Diary noted: "The excellence of the wine is dependent upon the site, but also upon the late harvesting." In 1885, Heinrich Wilhelm Dahlen compiled a map for the classification of the vineyards and for the taxes connected with them. The Charta association, founded in 1984, took up this idea and classified for their members the top quality sites of the Rheingau "as the areas known since ancient times as the best of all the sites." Wines from these sites produced according to fixed production directives were allowed to display the designation "Erstes Gewächs in accordance with the principles of the Charta". In order to attain legal status for the classification, a quality-map for the Rheingau was compiled together with the research institute in Geisenheim. In 1999, under the leadership of their association, the winemakers of the Rheingau became the first German wine region to step into this new territory (see also pages 42–44).

MITTELRHEIN

Total vine area: 472 hectares

Riesling: 323 hectares, represents 68.4% of the vine areas in the region, 1.1% of all German vine areas, 1% worldwide

High above the river, on picturesque wine terraces alongside mediaeval castles and palaces, the vineyards cling to the steep slopes of the Mittelrhein, a Rhine-and-wine landscape that was declared a World Cultural Heritage site in 2003 by UNESCO. However, this idyll conceals a full-blown crisis, with which above all winemaking on steeply sloping sites has been confronted for years. The time-consuming manual labor is cost-intensive and can no longer even begin to be compensated for by the attainable prices. Until about 100 years ago more than 2,000 hectares were cultivated here, today the figure is not quite 500 hectares. About three quarters of the area is planted with Riesling vines. Each year more areas remain uncultivated and more and more small businesses give up.

YOUTHFUL RENAISSANCE

Nevertheless, it is particularly the young winemakers who offer a future for wine production and the old cultural landscape along the Mittelrhein. The wine scene in what is in fact one of Germany's smallest growing regions is today defined by a handful of small, dedicated family businesses led by Florian Weingart, Matthias Müller, Jochen Katzenberger and Jens Diedinger. A stimulus and an example of this new winemaking generation was Peter Jost from the Hahnenhof in Bacharach who, at the beginning of the 1990s with his consistently quality-conscious winemaking, awoke the Mittelrhein to reality from its long sleep. Some have followed him, and instead of producing basis wines for the sparkling-hock industry or cheap swill for Romantic-Rhine tourism, the Mittelrhein winemakers of today are demonstrating what can be created from their soils.

ELEGANCE FROM STONE

In the stony slate and greywacke soils, Riesling finds a growing medium that bestows it with a racy character, fine fruity acidity and always a mineral touch. In good years, the light residual-sweet Rieslings in particular shine with a mineral elegance rarely found in Germany. Dry, in their youth the wines come across as somewhat reserved, because the acidity is still very marked. With increasing age they begin to gain in complex fruit aromas and in an elegant maturity.

RHEINHESSEN

Total vine area: 26,177 hectares
Riesling: 2,722 hectares, represents 10.3%
of the vine areas in the region,
9.0% of all German vine areas,
8.1% worldwide

The contradictions surrounding the largest German winegrowing region already begin with the name: Rheinhessen lies not in the federal state of Hesse, but in the Rhineland-Palatinate. For a long time Rheinhessen was the problem child in the German wine scene. The enormous sea of vines lacked a proper wine identity, there was hardly a grape variety which was not to be found in Rheinhessen earth, including almost all the new German crossings. Fields and meadows were often turned into vineyards without consideration for soil qualities or climatic conditions. In addition there was the almost cult-like burden of Rheinhessen export hits like "Blue Nun" and "Liebfraumilch" in all variations, which were often blamed squarely on the region.

A REVIVAL

In relation to the total vine area, there were only a few top class wine producers in Rheinhessen. Along with some quality producers directly on the Rhine in Nierstein and Oppenheim – Heyl zu Herrnsheim, St. Anthony and Schneider – it was above all Fritz Hasselbach from the Gunderloch estate in Nacken-

The Rote Hang facing the Rhine at Nierstein is one of the best-known sites in Rheinhessen

heim who at the end of the 1980s was the talk of the town with his quality Rieslings. Klaus Keller in Flörsheim-Dalsheim followed some years later by producing top-quality wines from unknown sites and thereby dumbfounding the experts. At the end of the 1990s in Westhofen, when the young Philipp Wittmann caused a furore with his elegant Rieslings, Rheinhessen experienced something like a resurrection. In the meantime, some other committed winemakers such as Gerhard Gutzler, Michael Pfannebecker, Erich Manz, Klaus Scherner and Daniel Wagner have joined the list, and, full of a sense of achievement, have spruced up the image of the region. Rheinhessen is beginning to tap its full climatic and soil-structural potential. The preconditions are really not bad. The soils offer lime and loess in the Rheinhessen hill-country, which is protected from cold winds by the Palatinate hills, as well as the Hunsrück and Taunus ranges. On the steep slopes of the terraces alongside the former course of the Rhine, elegant and complex Rieslings grow on red alluvial deposits of perlite and shale. Above all, the Roter Hang site near Nierstein is known for its corpulent, yet still elegant Rieslings.

PFALZ (PALATINATE)
Total vine area: 23,413 hectares
Riesling: 4,799 hectares, represents
20.5% of the vine areas in the region,
15.9% of all German vine areas,
14.3% worldwide

Germany's second-largest wine-growing region is only slightly smaller than neighboring Rheinhessen and from its southern limit at Worms extends over 50 miles across to the French border. The narrow Pfalz grape-belt runs parallel to the Rhine, although it does not directly reach its banks at any place. The mild climate, the protection from cold winds by the Palatine Forest, and relatively little rainfall allow a long ripening period for the grapes. The growing area is sub-divided into the areas of the Südliche Weinstrasse and Mittelhaardt, and the dividing line runs through Neustadt an der Weinstrasse.

THE HEART OF THE PFALZ
Nowhere else in the German growing regions do the vineyards lie so cheek-by-jowl as on the outer edge of the Haardt, the low foothills of the Palatine Forest. The mild climate imparts an almost Mediterranean character to this sweep of country. Where almonds, figs and citrus fruits ripen on the wind-protected slopes, Riesling also finds suitable conditions

for growth. The fertile soil, interspersed with loess, variegated sandstone, muschelkalk, marl, granite and shale, is reflected in all its variants in the character of the Pfalz Rieslings. In the Unterhaardt in the north, calciferous soils are to be found, which generate vigorous, meaty Rieslings. Along with those wine estates rich in tradition, such as Karl Schäfer and Pfeffingen-Fuhrmann-Eymael, here also Bernd Philippi, the Knipser brothers, Axel Neiss and Jochen Schmitt in Bad Dürkheim are the best interpreters of Riesling.

The Mittelhaardt possesses a great Riesling tradition. 80% of the many top sites around Deidesheim, Wachenheim and Forst are planted with this variety. Also the tradition of botrytized Pfalz Riesling has its origins here and reaches back to the year 1811. As well as the three great 'B's – Dr. von Bassermann-Jordan, Dr. Bürklin-Wolf and Reichsrat von Buhl – renowned family businesses such as Christmann and Mosbacher are also setting today's Riesling course.

THE SOUTH
In the area of the Südliche Weinstrasse, the vines grow largely in loam and loess soils. At the same time one finds weathered soils of variegated sandstone and muschelkalk, and in the southern Pfalz – for instance in the Kastanienbusch site – even red alluvial deposits or red shale.

NEW MOMENTUM
As in no other German wine growing region, Pfalz wine estates, after a weak period in the 1980s, have worked their way up into the German and international Riesling supergroup and have re-interpreted the style of the great, dry, elegant, complex Riesling. The spiritual leader of this Pfalz-comeback and the task-

As early as 1828 the Forster Ungeheuer site was assessed as a top-quality site according to Bavarian soil classification

master of an entire winemaker generation was Hans-Günther Schwarz, who as manager of the Müller-Catoir estate in the Haardt, produced fruity and expressive Rieslings which achieved the highest recognition at home and abroad. He was followed by well-trained winemakers who ensured a dynamic, further development and brought a notion of quality into many family businesses, in particular, Hansjörg Rebholz who caused a furore with his dry mineral Rieslings from the southern Pfalz. The duo of Uli Mell and Gunther Hauck brought the time-honored flagship of Bassermann-Jordan back into shape, and long-established family businesses such as Christmann, Mosbacher, Bergdolt, Weegmül-ler, Wilhelmshof and Wehrheim followed with remarkable Riesling qualities. At the same time, Christian von Guradze with his terroir concept set the course in the Bürklin-Wolf estate. Particularly in the last few years, this dynamic departure has borne much fruit. With young winemakers such as Volker Gies, Boris Kranz, Gerd Faubel, Markus Pfaffmann, Philipp Kuhn, Axel Neiss, Jochen Schmitt, Tina Pfaffmann and Markus Schneider, the Pfalz has talented new blood at its disposal.

NAHE

Total vine area: 4,145 hectares
Riesling: 1,031 hectares, represents
24.9% of the vine areas in the region,
3.4% of all German vine areas,
3.1% worldwide

For a long time, Nahe stood in the shadow of its great neighbors, Rheingau and Mosel. Until 1930, Nahe wines were largely still sold as Rhine wines. Only in 1971 were the boundaries of the growing region set down, and despite its diversity Nahe slowly received its own profile and a new self-confidence. Where top-quality Rieslings are concerned, middle-sized family businesses such as Dönnhoff, Emrich-Schönleber and Schlossgut Diel have been reliable guarantors of quality for years. Above all Helmut Dönnhoff caused an uproar at home and abroad with his sensational Rieslings. The top group has been followed for years by dedicated businesses such as Dr. Crusius, Kruger-Rumpf, Staatsdomäne Niederhausen and those estates where the next dedicated generation is already at the helm, such as Schäfer-Fröhlich, Hexamer, Korell, Tesch and Schweinhardt.

A MULTI-TALENT

What is typical about the Nahe region is that there is nothing typical about it. Indeed, the region is geographically and sensorily a multi-talent that allows a balancing act between a fine, tender style and a somewhat more compact, elegant style. The flavor nuances of the Rieslings can be very diverse, thanks to the continually varying soil structure: In the north, on a broad strip of quartzite, slate soils and greywacke soils grow fresh and racy wines. Further south, in the direction of Bad Kreuznach, sand, marl, loess and loam can be found which produces more finely flowery and elegant growths. To the west and north of the mid-Nahe, red shale defines the soil. The wines here are especially flowery and enduring, and have a discreet acidity. In the immediate area of the Nahe between Bad Münster and Schloss Böckelheim the terroir is of vol-canic origin and consists of porphyry. The Rieslings from these soils demonstrate a good deal of spice and fine mineral tones.

HESSISCHE BERGSTRASSE
Total vine area: 441 hectares
Riesling: 221 hectares, represents
50.1% of the vine areas in the region,
0.7% of all German vine areas,
0.7% worldwide

This small wine region between Darmstadt and Heppenheim, which only received its status of an independent growing area in 1971, offers winemaking some exceptional geological features as well as a very mild climate. While the Odenwald ridge protects the vine from cold winds, the vineyards enjoy optimal exposure to direct sunlight on the relatively steep slopes. The higher vineyards have soils of barren rock, granite, sandstone and lime, while further down, the soils are more fertile thanks to a humus layer. Riesling finds ideal conditions here; half of the growing area is planted with it. Apart from the Staatsweingut Bergstrasse, which time and again achieves botrytized Rieslings, there are only a few larger estates. The majority of wines is sold within the region by part-time winemakers.

FRANKEN (FRANCONIA)
Total vine area: 6,051 hectares
Riesling: 263 hectares, represents
4.3% of the vine areas in the region,
0.9% of all German vine areas,
0.8% worldwide

This winegrowing region extends along the Main river from Aschaffenburg to Hassfurt. In a wine sense, Franken is known more for its traditional Silvaner than for Riesling which accordingly only takes up a small proportion of the total vine area. The world of Riesling is small here; among its best-known protagonists are Paul Fürst in Bürgstadt, Robert Haller from the Weingut Fürst Löwenstein, of course Horst Sauer, Martin Steinmann from Schloss Sommerhausen, Dr. Heinrich Wirsching in Iphofen, Schmitt's Kinder in Randersacker and the young Ludwig Knoll from Würzburg. In the heart of the growing area, the Main triangle in and around Würzburg, Rieslings grow in muschelkalk soils that impart into the wines an earthy tone full of character. In the Steigerwald zone around Kitzingen, the vines are in fertile keuper, muschelkalk, loamy loess and at Iphofen even in schilfsandstein. Along the lower Main river between Aschaffenburg and Miltenberg, a different geology and a milder climate prevail. In the western zone, on the steep slopes along the small Kahl river or in the superb Homburger Kallmuth, some of the most interesting Franconian Rieslings grow on variegated sandstone and shell sandstone.

BADEN

Total vine area: 15,977 hectares
Riesling: 1,228 hectares, represents
7.7% of the vine areas in the region,
4.1% of all German vine areas,
3.7% worldwide

The most southerly German winegrowing region is the only one that belongs to the EU's winegrowing-zone B and thus to the same climate zone as Alsace and the Loire. Riesling vineyards are only sporadically to be found. In the Ihringer Winklerberg on the Kaiserstuhl, the variety must prove that it can develop well on volcanic, rocky ground alongside Pinot varieties. Some of Baden's best Rieslings

grow in Ortenau on steep slopes covered with weathered granite. The best site is Plauelrain in Durbach, which in good years yields the entire quality palette, including ice wine. However, the Badische Bergstrasse is also known for its racy Rieslings which grow on the steep slopes, in a weathered soil formed of primitive rocks. It was small and middle-sized family businesses such as Andreas Laible, Schloss Neuweier, Dr. Heger and Gut Nägelsförst that in the last few decades have brought Baden's Rieslings up to quality.

WÜRTTEMBERG

Total vine area: 11,522 hectares
Riesling: 2,143 hectares, represents 18.6%
of the vine areas in the region,
7.1% of all German vine areas,
6.4% worldwide

Red Trollinger is not the only wine grown in Württemberg. In fact, up to one fifth of the considerable vine area is planted with Riesling. The fact that even now little is heard about Württemberg Rieslings is because most of the wines produced are marketed by co-operatives and directly consumed within the region. On the other hand there are only a few businesses that concentrate on the production of top-quality Rieslings. This group includes the long-established estates of Graf Adelmann, Fürst zu Hohenlohe-Öhringen, Karl Haidle, Gerhard Aldinger and Ernst Dautel, but also aspiring newcomers: Rainer Schnaitmann, Jochen Beurer and Hans-Peter Wöhrwag. The winegrowing center lies between Heilbronn and Stuttgart. The Riesling vines grow in a fertile soil of keuper and muschelkalk. In the Rems valley, Rieslings grow alongside Trollinger, Kerner and Silvaner on southern slopes and usually display a pithy acidity.

ALSACE

Riesling country between two cultures

Riesling cultivation-zone latitudes:
48° to 49° N.
Total vine area: 15,230 hectares
Riesling: 3,355 hectares,
represents 22.0% of Alsatian vine areas,
10.0% worldwide
Main risks for viticulture:
soil erosion, water shortage
Average temperature in July: 19°C

RIESLING, WHERE CULTURES MEET

Embedded between the Vosges Mountains and the heights of the Black Forest opposite, the Alsatian vine slopes stretch for almost 65 miles from Strasbourg into the region around Mulhouse (see map on page 38). What the Romans had already noticed as they advanced up the Rhône into Alsace with their armies is still of benefit to winemaking today: the relatively mild, semi-continental climate with sunny, warm and dry weather. Riesling has been cultivated here for centuries. Particularly in the last three decades its growing areas have been expanded, above all at the expense of Sylvaner.

The variety profits from the many hours of sunshine in the months of May through October, the slow ripening period encourages the development of the fine aromas and allows the extract values in the grapes to increase. In some years, a relatively high humidity in the fall facilitates noble rot. Accordingly, the palette extends from simple wines-by-the-glass to dry, mineral-characterized Rieslings with a lot of body and structure or botrytis-characterized wines to complex botrytized specialties.

EXOTIC RIESLING

In the French wine world, the Rieslings from the départements of Haut-Rhin and Bas-Rhin which constitute Alsace are largely considered as exotics, for the taste of Alsatian Riesling is neither one thing nor the other: the wines of this border region are not quite French and not quite German.

The mixture of history, culture and tradition here has also brought about an individual character in Riesling. Thus, the turbulent history of Alsace is reflected in its wine: continual ups and downs in a border region that even well into the 20th century was a bone of contention between France and Germany. Only after World War II was Alsace able to find a new identity and thereby also a consistent quality policy in winemaking.

The Alsatian wine landscape at the intersection of two cultures

PROTAGONISTS OF SUCCESS

An assurance of this was provided not only by those estates rich in tradition, such as Hugel et Fils in Riquewihr, Trimbach in Ribeauvillé with their rare Riesling Clos Ste Hune or the world-famous Domaine Zind-Humbrecht in Turckheim. In the last two decades, smaller family businesses have also influenced the new face of Alsace with their mostly or-ganically produced wines. First and foremost André Ostertag in Epfig, Marc Kreydenweiss in Andlau and the unflagging defender of terroir-typical wines Jean-Michel Deiss in Bergheim, to name but a few.

TERROIR MOSAIC

The terroir upon which they all work offers a potential for great Rieslings, and the soils in all their diversity form a geological mosaic which is difficult to find anywhere else in the world. Between 47° and 49° N., there are at least 20 different soil formations from a num-ber of geologic eras, from granite to gneiss, slate, lime, sandstone, sand and loess right up to muschelkalk and volcanic ash. The majori-ty of vineyards are to be found at a height of between 175 and 420 meters above sea level and lie in the foothills of the Vosges on layers of sediment. In northern Alsace, well-mixed soils containing lime and marl are to be found, which rather tends toward quite broad Ries-lings. Some famous terroirs such as the Schlossberg beneath the Kaysersberg and the Wineck-Schlossberg are on granite soils. These are coarse-grained and sandy, but at the same time rich in mineral nutrients. Particu-larly fine Rieslings grow here with an abun-dance of aromas and a discreet mineral note. On the higher and steeper sites of the Vosges a thinner topsoil lies over weathered gneiss, granite, sandstone, slate and various volcanic deposits. Flint and slate make themselves par-ticularly noticeable with Riesling; they give

the wines a characteristic mineral aroma which, with maturity, is reminiscent of petroleum. The lower slopes of the Vosges owe their existence to the valley of the original course of the Rhine. Here a deeper topsoil lies on clay, marl, limestone and sandstone. The plain at the foot of the Vosges consists largely of alluvial land, mostly sandy and stony soils which are however deep and permeable and produce by contrast simple Rieslings.

APPELLATION D'ORIGINE CONTRÔLÉE

All Alsatian wines belong to one of the three "controlled appellations of origin" (Appellation d'origine contrôlée – AOC): Alsace, Alsace Grand Cru (complemented with the name of one of 50 delimited sites which are allowed in the appellation) and additionally Crémant d'Alsace (sparkling wine, usually produced on the basis of Pinot Blanc and in accordance with the traditional method).

AOC Alsace

The Alsatian AOC wines originate – usually 100% – from one variety which must be declared on the label. The maximum permitted yield of 100 hectoliters per hectare is set higher than in all other appellations. If there is no declaration given, then an assemblage of various varieties is involved, sometimes called "Edelzwicker", sometimes also accompanied by "Gentil" or with a brand name. The current mandatory minimum alcohol content is 9.5% for Riesling.

AOC Alsace Grand Cru

The 50 Alsatian Grand Cru sites were set down in 1975 by the Institut National des Appellations d'Origine (INAO) with consideration for geological and microclimatic particularities. Grand Cru wines are allowed to be produced only from the varieties Riesling, Gewürztraminer, Tokay Pinot Gris or Muscat d'Alsace. Since 2001, the vineyards must be planted with at least 4,500 vines per hectare, the basic yield is set at a maximum of 55 hectoliters per hectare, and the grapes must be picked by hand. The minimum alcohol content for Riesling is 11%. In order to be certified as Appellation Alsace Grand Cru the wines must undergo prior tasting under supervision of the INAO and must be produced exclusively from the variety in question.

Vendange tardive

Previously, the winemaker was allowed to choose which designation he gave to his wines: Spätlese, Auslese or Beerenauslese. Since 1983 a Vendange tardive, as late-harvest wines are known in French, may only be pressed from varieties that are authorized for Grands Crus. Chaptalization is not allowed, the minimum sugar content must amount to 220 grams per liter (95° Oechsle) for Riesling, the harvesting may only take place within a specified time period and must be declared so that an official control can take place. A Vendange tardive need not be beset with botrytis.

Sélection des grains nobles

This is a Vendange tardive in which the classic Grand Cru varieties are allowed. The minimum sugar content must amount to 256 grams per liter (110° Oechsle) for Riesling, and the same rules apply as with a Vendange tardive. Since it requires considerable experience to produce such complex wines, quality and price often unfortunately diverge quite considerably.

OTHER REGIONS IN EUROPE

The courage to take risks

Outside of the classic growing areas, Riesling appears only very sporadically in almost all the world's wine regions, often only as the dalliance of an ambitious winemaker or as an experiment with insignificant quantities.

LUXEMBOURG

In Luxembourg there are currently about 160 hectares planted with Riesling. The soils range from muschelkalk in canton Grevenmacher, to loamy keuper soils in canton Remich. In terms of style, Luxembourgeois Rieslings are reminiscent of simple Mosel wines, they often have an accent of carbon dioxide, but are usually picked too early and then exhibit a touch of unripeness. However, there are some committed winemakers such as Abi Duhr, who wrest complex, high-quality Rieslings from nature. The best producers are Clos des Rochers and Château Pauqué in Grevenmacher, Thill Frères in Schengen, Domaine Bastian in Remich, Domaine Aly Duhr in Ahn, Domaine Alice Hartmann in Wormeldange and Domaines Charles Decker and Sunnen-Hoffmann, both in Remerschen.

ITALY

In the white-wine portfolio of Italy, Riesling plays only a subordinate role. The so-called

Rheinriesling, which one finds above all in the north, is cultivated in small quantities in Trentino, Lombardy, Veneto, Friuli and in

The pergola training system is widespread in Italy and ensures a consistent canopy of leaves

South Tyrol. About 35 hectares are currently planted with Riesling in South Tyrol, the vineyards rising to an altitude of 500 meters above sea level. The variety can be found above all in the winemaking communities of Margreid, Kurtinig, Eppan and Neumarkt. The best representatives certainly come from the relatively cool Eisack valley and from Vinschgau. Since 2002, the former has had its own DOC designation Eisack-Riesling. South Tyrol Rieslings are as a rule dry and display a highly individual character. The tangy acidity is often somewhat to the fore; the wines are usually slim and elegant, with less body and richness.

SPAIN

In Penedès, Miguel Torres produces, alongside Riesling-Cuvées and a simple basic wine, a Riesling which he has named after his wife. Waltraut-Riesling is a juicy, light residual-sugar wine with pleasant acidity and about 13% alcohol.

PORTUGAL

Dirk Niepoort fosters a personal love for Riesling. Recently he was able to acquire a vineyard in the Douro Valley at a height of 800 meters above sea level. The weathered slate soil affords the roots the possibility to penetrate deep into the earth in order to extract minerals. The first Nieport Riesling was lacking somewhat in harmony, but those who know Dirk Niepoort's vigorous ambition can imagine what could still become of this Riesling project.

SWITZERLAND

It may be quite astounding to some, in view of the difficult terrain in this Alpine country and the consequent high price of production, to hear that Switzerland is also a wine country. Winemaking is practiced in every Swiss canton, and with about 10 hectares of vines, Riesling is only one exotic amongst many.

EASTERN EUROPE

The wine history of the Danubian countries Hungary, Bulgaria, Romania and Slovenia stretches way back in time. Nevertheless, half a century of communism not only cut off the markets in the West, but at the same time inhibited investment and reduced production to cheap bulk wine. There are some signs of awakening, and usually investors from the Western wine nations are behind them. In Slovakia, on the border to Hungary, the Egon Müller-Scharzhof estate is involved in cultivating dry Rieslings all around the stately home of Baron Ullmann. Around 25,000 bottles of Château Béla come on to the market every year.

According to information from experts, many thousands of hectares of Riesling exist in the countries of the former Soviet Union. Nevertheless, it is not yet verified whether they are actually cases of genetically genuine Riesling. It remains to be seen how these areas will develop agriculturally and whether winemaking will attain in future anything more than national importance.

SOUTH AMERICA/ CHILE

The Torres estate produces here a simple, light cuvée of Gewürztraminer and Riesling.

AUSTRIA

A newcomer rich in tradition

Riesling cultivation-zone latitudes:
47° to 48° N.
Total vine area: 48,500 hectares
Riesling: 1,624 hectares, represents 3.3% of all Austrian vine areas, 4.8% worldwide
Wachau: Total vine area: 1,390 hectares
Riesling: 185 hectares, represents 13.3% of the vine areas in the region, 11.4% of all Austrian vine areas, 0.6% worldwide

Kamptal: Total vine area: 3,867 hectares
Riesling: 298 hectares, represents 7.7% of the vine areas in the region, 18.3% of all Austrian vine areas, 0.9% worldwide
Kremstal: Total vine area: 2,170 hectares
Riesling: 186 hectares, represents 8.6% of the vine areas in the region, 11.5% of all Austrian vine areas, 0.6% worldwide
Main risks for viticulture: late frost
Average temperature in July: 20°C

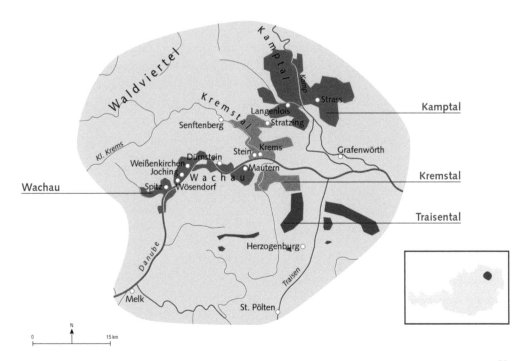

RETROSPECTIVE

In Austria one can look back almost three millennia and discover traces of wine at every turn. Celts, Romans and above all Charlemagne promoted winemaking. Over the centuries, there were ups and downs time and again. However, the best thing to befall Austrian winemaking in the last 50 years was the diethylene glycol scandal of 1985. This massive collapse of the marketing structures and the precipitous loss of image forced Austria's winemakers to make an unconditional new start in a consistent way, which guaranteed quality without restriction.

COMEBACK

Today, Austria presents itself as a wine country with a very independent profile, and Austrian wines are more in demand and enjoy better repute than in all the years previously. Austria, too, plays in the world's great wine orchestra, at least in terms of quality. As far as quantity goes, Austria produces only about one percent of the world's wines.

The recognizable increase in quality is due on the one hand to the tightening of the wine law in 1985 – as a consequence of the scandal – and on the other hand, to the founding of many brand communities such as the Vinea Wachau, which has imposed strict controls on its members. The most modern wine-estate architecture is to be found in all Austrian winemaking regions, a visible sign of a community of winemakers geared to the future and who fulfill their tradition with new, youthful life.

AN IDEAL CLIMATE

The winemakers use the climatic and geologic conditions of the growing areas for the production of high-quality wines. The wine areas lie in temperate climate zones without extremes between 47° and 48° N., comparable for example with Burgundy in France. Warm summers with many hours of sunshine during the day and long, mild autumnal days with cool nights are typical of the majority of Austrian winemaking regions.

NEVER WITHOUT RIESLING

Austria offers a great diversity of wine varieties, which take account of the varying soils and climates. About ten red and twenty white wine varieties are cultivated, among these also Riesling. However, only in Kremstal, Kamptal and above all in Wachau does it have a real importance. In all three areas, the vineyard soils are largely characterized by primitive rocks.

WACHAU

Deeply imbedded in the primitive rock, the Danube winds its way through the Wachau. Gneiss, granulite and mica slate sets the tone in the area between Spitz and Krems and turn the barren soils of the Bohemian Massif into the resonating body of the wines which grow here. From the northern wooded areas come the cool winds, which in the valley of Wachau meet with the milder currents from the Pannonian Plain. A noticeable change between warm days and cool nights creates the optimum climatic rhythm, which conditions the wary ripeness of the grapes.

The relatively long period on the vine is an elemental factor which always makes the Wachau Rieslings a little spicier, smoother and more complex. Even with the light, fresh wines this spicy fruit-interplay of peach and apricot is convincing. These monumental, even sublime wines present themselves correspondingly more luscious, with an almost ly, the grapes further north in the sediment soils in the Chehalem Mountains achieve an earlier ripening.

The winegrowing area experienced its upturn from the 1960s with the Pinot Noir variety; almost half of the vine areas in Willamette Valley being planted with this, the grape that makes red Burgundies. Riesling could never fully gain a foothold in Oregon, although Riesling vines, above all in the north of the valley, in Washington County, have produced better qualities than Chardonnay. At present, Riesling has few chances against Pinot Gris and Pinot Noir, it is unpopular, although it would flourish wonderfully on the higher slopes of Willamette Valley with relatively low temperatures. However, there are some wineries, such as Amity Vineyards, Argyle, Elk Cove and Scott Henry Estate, which have, alongside Pinot Noir, also devoted themselves to Riesling.

NEW YORK

New York is the third-largest vine-growing state in the USA, although more than half of the production is used for grape juice and similar products. The bulk of the vineyards is younger than fifteen years old, the majority of wineries is situated around the Finger Lakes, south of Lake Ontario. Very significant here for winemaking are Lakes Canandaigua, Keuka, Seneca and Cayuga, because they exert a moderating effect on the climate and thereby allow the formation of botrytis. Commercial winemaking has been practiced here since the mid-19th century on about 4,000 hectares of really deep and water-permeable soils with a continental climate.

The winters can be long and unrelentingly cold, and temperatures often fall to -20°C. The relatively hardy Riesling therefore is among the preferred varieties on the Finger Lakes, even if it only constitutes 5% of the vine area. Here also, thanks to the temperatures, the production of ice wine is possible, and it is allowed – in contrast to Germany and Canada – to bring the grapes or the must down to freezing point. Above all, the following wineries are noteworthy: Heron Hill, Hosmer, Lamoreaux, Vinifera Wine Cellars and Hermann J. Wiemer, who is known for his dry Riesling reminiscent of a Nahe in wine style.

CALIFORNIA

In the 1960s Riesling was one of the most-grown grape varieties in California, but had already lost ground again by the 1970s. Today, Californian Riesling is if anything a scarce commodity. No wonder: the temperatures are far too high for the variety, and in those places where their cultivation would be worthwhile, one finds the dominant Chardonnay. In addition, many wineries in Washington have depressed the market for off-dry Riesling into an absolutely cheap price category, and have thereby made it unprofitable.

There are however, a few winemakers who do not wish to do without the variety completely. Their Riesling sites are found in the cooler or higher regions, and they have devoted themselves rather more to the botrytis-characterized late-harvest process. These include classic winegrowers such as Joseph Phelps, Freemark Abbey, Chateau St. Jean, Trefethen and Smith-Madrone, but also the wild-boy winemaker Randall Graham from Bonny Doon winery, who has devoted himself to a completely different method in Santa Cruz. He produces a multicultural cuvée on the Australian pattern with American Riesling from Washington and California and German Mosel Riesling from Johannes Selbach.

CANADA

Ice wine power

Riesling cultivation-zone latitudes:
48° to 49° N.
Total vine area: 9,000 hectares
Riesling: 440 hectares, represents
4.9% of all Canadian vine areas,
1.3% worldwide
Main risks for viticulture:
insufficient ripening, frost
Average temperature in July: 18°C

This enormous country is known above all for its relatively cool climate. Nevertheless, wine-making is practiced in four different provinces. Alongside vine slopes in Quebec and Nova Scotia in the southeast, and British Columbia, the majority of Canadian wines – about 80% – come from Ontario province (see map on page 63).

The beginnings of Canadian winemaking lie in the early 19th century: up until the 1970s above all sweet, high-alcohol wines were produced from native, hardy wine varieties such as Seyval Blanc and Vidal, which were marketed as "Sherry" or "Port". Only in the 1980s did European varieties such as Chardonnay, Riesling, Pinot Noir and Cabernet Sauvignon start to be planted in Canada on an increasing scale. More and more importance is being attached to good quality, and the proportion of European varieties continues to rise; today,

the figure is already 40%. In Okanagan, successful experiments with Syrah and other varieties continue to be made. Each year, 100 to 500 hectares are newly planted and mostly with European varieties.

In Canada, Riesling is produced in the German style: dry, off-dry, late harvest wines as a rule sweet, but principally as ice wine. Canada is the largest ice wine producer in the world and regularly receives high honors at international wine awards. Official regulations and standards are strictly controlled, and artificial freezing – in contrast to the USA – is no longer permitted. Since July 1, 2004 there exists a bilateral accord between Canada and Germany, which in mutual agreement permits the production of ice wine only from natural yields frozen on the vine. The annual production is almost one million bottles. 75% of ice wines are produced from the hybrid variety Vidal, which creates rather jammy wines but is the actual moneymaker. Nevertheless, the proportion of Riesling continually grows, because it is in a much better position to concentrate the aromas in the grape and to express them more intricately on a noticeably higher quality level.

ONTARIO

The majority of vineyards are to be found on the climatically favored Niagara Peninsula. This narrow strip of land with its sandy loam

grapes are pressed into wine, the rest being marketed as table grapes, or processed into must concentrate or raisins, or distilled. With a 1% portion of the world's total vine areas, South Africa is only in 20th place among wine-making countries, but its annual production of 10 million hectoliters puts it in eighth place. The mass production in some areas allows yields of up to 220 hectoliters per hectare. In addition there exists quality winemaking, which was already producing fresh, fruity wines with a temperature-controlled fermentation technique in the 1950s. In 1973 the "Wine of Origin" laws were passed – following the French AOC system – which offered the consumer a quality orientation. Not until 1985 was the first barrel-fermented Chardonnay produced in Paarl; to this day, this variety is one of the South Africa's flagship wines.

The Cape region is South Africa's most fascinating wine landscape

COOL CLIMATE

The striving for quality is leading ever more often to a rethinking. The realization that mass production is negative, and the decision to plant the variety most suitable for the soils available, are what today determine many new plantings. Cooler sites are in demand, since above all the summer temperatures are higher than in the classic Riesling regions of Europe.

COASTAL REGIONS

Along the south coast, the areas of Constantia, Elgin, Walker Bay and Hermanus profit from the Cape Doctor, a cool and powerful south-easterly wind, and sometimes it seriously lashes the vines. However, it forces out the high humidity and thus the mildew as well as other undesirable fungal diseases. The vineyards of the coastal regions are situated higher and are considerably cooler than vine areas in the middle of the valleys. The soils are very variable, in the south at Constantia granite and sandstone dominate, in Elgin there is even slate.

THE HEART OF WINEMAKING

The center of South African winemaking is Stellenbosch. The leading estates and Riesling protagonists are based here. Hermann Kirschbaum, a winemaker from Buitenverwachting, loves Riesling in the style of the Mosel. Gyles Webb, one of the best winemakers in South Africa, produces each year remarkable Rieslings in the Thelema Mountain Vineyards. The husband-and-wife team of Gary and Cathy Jordan have planted their Riesling at an elevation of 300 meters in weathered granite soil. However, South Africa's real Riesling freak is Dan de Wet from the De Wetshof Estate in Robertson. He studied in Geisenheim, Germany, and today produces three different Riesling types which are worth trying.

SOUTH AFRICA

Cape of New Riesling Hope

Riesling cultivation-zone latitudes:
33° to 34° S.
Total vine area: 129,000 hectares
Riesling: 347 hectares, represents
0.3% of all South African vine areas,
1.0% worldwide
Main risks for viticulture:
vine diseases
Average temperature in January: 23°C

As in no other country, the moment of birth of winemaking on the Cape can be determined to the exact day. Seven years after Jan van Riebeeck first stood on South African soil on behalf of the Dutch East India Company on April 6, 1652, the first must flowed out of the press. In 1685 the next governor, Simon van der Stel, founded the legendary Constantia estate which had a considerable influence on winemaking on the Cape. In the 18th century the Muscat dessert wines of Constantia were in demand throughout Europe at a time when estates such as Lafite and Roma-née-Conti were still in their infancy. There followed highs and lows until well into the 20th century. Only with the end of apartheid in 1994 did South Africa become a modern, open wine country and today she plays a decisive role on the world's wine market. The climatic conditions on the Cape are ideal, and most vines enjoy almost Mediterranean conditions. Originally, irrigation was relied upon. Today however there are in the cooler areas such as Constantia, Stellenbosch and Elgin some vineyards which have renounced irrigation. The vine roots do not press so deep into the soil with regular irrigation and therefore they cannot reach the important minerals. The cold Benguela Current ensures that it is cooler on the Cape than one would expect from this latitude.

THE RIESLING OF THE IMMIGRANTS

Along with Dutch seafarers and Huguenots, it is the Germans whose influence in South Africa is discernible. Many South African winemakers and young, ambitious viticulturalists have studied wine growing in Germany and there discovered their love of Riesling. This is why the variety has a secure place, but its proportion of the whole vine area has noticeably receded in the last ten years. After a short-lived heyday with 1600 hectares in the 1990s, Riesling has today been reduced to an area of 350 hectares and plays only a subordinate role in South Africa's white-wine portfolio.

BULK AND QUALITY

South Africa has more winemaking land at its disposal than Australia. Only a portion of the

NORTH ISLAND

Hawkes Bay

South-west of Gisborne, one of New Zealand's oldest growing areas opens out. Hawkes Bay registers the second-highest duration of sunshine in the country. The vines are continually supplied with a cool sea breeze and are able to slowly mature into their ideal ripeness. Riesling grows on dry gravel soils, the wines are luscious, big, quite heavy and characterized by tropical fruit aromas.

Wairarapa/Martinborough

The official designation of the most southerly growing area of North Island is Wairarapa, more common however is Martinborough. Among the white varieties, Riesling is among the favorites; a lot of sun during the day and cool nights permit the creation of aromatic wines. The grapes of the primarily small estates grow in stony-dry, partly alluvial, but also loamy soils that produce low yields. The Dry River Riesling by Dr. Neil McCullum counts as one of New Zealand's finest and longest-living Rieslings.

SOUTH ISLAND

Marlborough

Long, sunny days, cool nights and in good years, a dry fall – these are the conditions for winemaking in Marlborough. However, the greatest potential is found in the gravel soils with a light loam layer in which the vines can put down deep roots. The water-permeable rock produces piquant, aromatic Sauvignon Blancs, but also fruit-rich Rieslings ranging all the way to luscious, sweet, botrytized late-harvest qualities.

Nelson

One of the youngest growing areas is found directly beside the Abel Tasman National Park. The – for the south – relatively high rainfall, and the fresh winds from Tasman Bay allow above all those varieties to grow which, during the ripening phase, prefer it to be somewhat cooler. Chardonnay dominates, Riesling grows in calciferous rock which lends the wines a crispy, aromatic character.

Canterbury and Central Otago

Canterbury, the aspiring growing area in the mid-east of South Island, is divided into two regions. The vineyards are situated all around the town of Christchurch in a cool plain, and in Wairapa – 40 minutes' drive from Christchurch – winemaking is practiced on gentle hills. The vines flourish in volcanic loess and chalk soils. Canterbury has become known for its Pinot Noirs, but also through Riesling. The cool climate accommodates the variety well. From simple table wine right up to botrytized specialties, one can find everything here. Among the most important Riesling producers are the Giesen brothers from Germany's Pfalz as well as Lynette Hudson and Matthew Donaldson with their residual-sweet Riesling Pegasus Bay.

The world's southernmost growing area, Central Otago, is the only region with a continental climate. This brings with it the risk of frost, but on the other hand there is little rainfall and accordingly many hours of sun with a long, dry fall period. The top producer is Felton Road. Winemaker Walter Blair is responsible for the finely-fruity, mineral pear-aromas of Rieslings with delicate acidity and a citrus character, which one could quite easily confuse with expressive Mosel Rieslings.

NEW ZEALAND

Riesling from the other end of the world

Riesling cultivation-zone latitudes:
41° to 42° S.; Marlborough
Total vine area: 18,000 hectares
Riesling: 636 hectares, represents
3.5% of all New Zealand vine areas,
1.9% worldwide
Main risks for viticulture:
rain, phylloxera
Average temperature in January: 18°C

Compared with other countries of the New World, New Zealand has hitherto remained a very small wine country. Although the first vines were already planted in 1819, a good 150 years later, in 1960, the country had only 400 hectares under vines. A large proportion of this was planted with Müller-Thurgau, since German analysts were of the opinion that Riesling on the South Island, specifically in Otago, would not flourish.

Finally, in the 1970s visionaries such as John Buck and the Spence brothers, began to plant vines from Burgundy and the Bordelais. However, only in the 1990s was there an expansion of quality winemaking on both islands. That was the start of the triumphal march of New Zealand's Sauvignon Blanc, which found ideal conditions here. Along with this development however, Riesling was also able to establish a foothold on both islands.

CLIMATE AND TERROIR

Characteristic of New Zealand is the relatively cool climate influenced by the cool currents of the Pacific Ocean and powerful, fresh west winds.

There exist quite noticeable climatic differences between the warmer North Island and the cooler South Island. Heavy rainfall encourages leaf and shoot growth and thereby also the grassy, green tones in the wine. This is why New Zealand has been able to develop a perfect canopy management, which has clearly been able to add to the improvement in wine quality.

On North Island, varying soil formations affect the character of the grape. While in Northland shallow clay soils prevail, one finds in Waikato heavy loam soils on clayey subsoil, around the town of Gisborne alluvial sand soils with volcanic additions and in Hawkes Bay, loam- and sand soils, mixed with gravelly rock or volcanic rock. The lightest soils are in the hinterland of Hastings.

On South Island the soil changes from loamy marl to hard, loamy, almost clayey subsoil. In contrast, in Central Otago nutrient-poor granite and slate soils predominate, with fine sand and loess dust triturated by the glaciers, an ideal precondition for Riesling. The variation between hot days and cool nights is quite extreme.

More and more vineyards are being established in the vastness of Australia

WESTERN AUSTRALIA

Western Australia, whose vineyards were laid out in the first half of the 19th century, is the largest state of the country, but the wine industry has developed only slowly in comparison with the other regions. The winters are usually cold and rainy, the summers on the other hand are hot with daytime temperatures around 32°C. In the night it becomes cooler, often down to 6°C. About 120 miles south of Perth is the Margaret River. Leeuwin Estate is the only estate to which an internationally recognized Riesling vineyard belongs. Noteworthy Rieslings are found in the cooler, continental climate of the Great Southern winemaking region, including Mount Barker and Frankland. With Isolation Ridge – which grows on gravelly loam and clay soils and imparts aromas with spicy, limey and mineral hints – Judi Cullam from the Frankland Estate has demonstrated that one can produce great Rieslings even under difficult conditions.

TASMANIA

Winemaking actually only began here in the 1970s, and the future will demonstrate what is to be achieved in this region.

The climate is cool, the ripening period long, the soils are of volcanic origin, and the climatic variations enhance the ripening of the grapes. As a rule, Tasmanian Rieslings taste light and flowery.

CHAPTER 3

SAVORING AND ITS MANY FACETS

THE RELATIONSHIP BETWEEN AROMA AND TERROIR

NATURE'S BUILDING-BLOCK SYSTEM

How do aromas get into the wine?

A LIBRARY OF AROMAS

Why does Riesling smell of citrus, apple and peach? Or even of wet stones, petroleum or smoke? Interestingly, nature has at its disposal a particular repertoire of chemical compounds which are responsible for smells and fragrances, and – for economic reasons, one could almost think – are deployed at the same time in various ways: in fruits, vegetables, plants and trees, and in flowers, grass and even in wine. Indeed, the vine originates from a common genealogy of plants, which in the course of evolution, has developed in various directions. Common features have remained, such as aromas, and therefore the same mercaptan compounds are to be found in passionfruit for example as in the Riesling grape, and almost identical monoterpenes are found in roses, lychees and Riesling.

Hitherto, about 800 chemical compounds have been identified in wines, which to a large degree are the same as those in well-known fruits. Our brains function as a kind of library of aromas that perform a sample comparison between the smells stored in one's memory and those being currently discerned by the nose. The more smells and fragrances that are stored, the better, more rapid and distinct will be the recall, the recognition and the assignment of these fragrance samples to the relevant verbal descriptions.

QUALITY REQUIRES RIPENING

Aromas are formed in a similar way to the red pigments of red wines in the grape skins, since they are dependent on photosynthesis, which transforms the sun's energy into energy-rich sugar. The decisive phase of the formation of aromas starts with the actual ripening process: once a certain amount of sugar has been produced and stored in the grape then it begins to form aromas, tannins and pigments. Precisely at the time when sugar build-up is changing only marginally, and must weight is stagnating, the grapes achieve their full aromatic maturity. It is just this which makes an involvement with Riesling so exciting, for, like no other type of white wine, it requires a long ripening phase on the vine in order to be able to fully develop its aromas.

The grape cannot itself make this diversity perceptible, for, as personal experience shows, different grape varieties differ less in flavor than the wines made from them. The majority of what are called flavor precursors formed in the grape cannot yet evaporate, and are thus unable to release a smell in the nose. It is not until fermentation that they are released, thereby forming the characteristic aroma of the grape variety. One important aspect of the operations in the cellar is the endeavor to cautiously liberate the dormant aroma-potential in the grapes. This also explains why wines made from unripe grapes always taste aromatically lean, since there are few flavor precursors formed within them to be released.

DIFFERENT CAUSES

Aromas in wine have various origins. For one thing there are the typical aromas from the grapes of each variety that are always found in the wine in a more or less intense and modified form. Other aromas arise during fermentation and are dependent upon the types of yeasts used – wild yeasts or cultured yeasts – and upon the fermentation temperature. Finally aromas arise during ripening and storage, and they can therefore also suggest the age of any particular Riesling. In order for us to be able to detect these aromas, the molecules need to be so small that they can evaporate. They should not be too easily soluble in water, since they would then hardly pass into the top of the wineglass and thus remain odorless like sugar or acid.

There is no absolute standard of how a fruit or a wine should always smell or to which a judgment could be geared: Each person has an individual ability to perceive, and this is why the same wine or the same fruit can be variously perceived by different individuals. Each of us can nevertheless imagine something by the

The decisive phase in the formation of aromas is initially set in motion by the actual ripening process

smell of an apple, the fragrance of a rose or the aroma of honey, and by thus referring to well-known odors, we facilitate communication about the diversity of Riesling.

On the following pages, we shall introduce to you the most important aromas which contribute in varying intensity to the olfactory make-up of Rieslings from all around the world.

AROMAS FROM THE GRAPE

APPLE

Just like Riesling, the apple also has a natural juiciness, which is supported by a refreshing acidity structure. This similarity makes the scent of an apple one of Riesling's basic aromatic attributes. Simple and very young Rieslings exhibit fresh, green, lightly grassy Granny-Smith tones, while in contrast, ripened growths are rather more reminiscent of the yellow-redolent, aroma-rich apple varieties such as Belle de Boskoop or Cox's Orange Pippin.

LEMON

The subtle, fruity aroma of the lemon is equally fundamental and is characteristic of almost all Rieslings. Although still quite apparent in young, fresh Rieslings, this aroma quality is less apparent in Rieslings of Auslese quality or above. This citrus-like aroma tends to be discernible in Rieslings from stony soils, such as for example in the Nahe and Saar regions, but also in Rieslings from the New World.

PEACH

Peach aromas are recognizable in Rieslings from rather cooler wine growing areas while they are still in an early stage of development. The wines growing on firm slate soils such as on the Wehlener Sonnenuhr site, on the steep slopes of Rüdesheim, along the Mittelrhein or along the Nahe, exhibit an aromatic profile reminiscent of juicy peaches.

APRICOT

Apricot aromas in wine usually smell somewhat riper and more concentrated than fine peach nuances. The smell of apricot is thus also a typical feature of Rieslings made with grapes harvested fully-ripe. A maceration period can particularly intensify this aroma. Rieslings from more substantial soils – such as, for instance in the Pfalz, in the upper Rheingau, in Wachau and Alsace – exhibit this intensive smell-of-apricots characteristic very distinctly. Surprisingly, apricot aromas are still perceivable when the Riesling grapes are affected by *Botrytis cinerea*.

PASSION-FRUIT

The aroma of this exotic fruit is noticeable above all in ripe wines of Spätlese quality and above, and is correspondingly a typical feature of botrytized Rieslings. The aroma of passion-fruit also characterizes Rieslings from warmer winegrowing regions and from lime-rich soils, as are to be found for instance in Alsace, in Rheinhessen and around the town of Bad Dürkheim. Passion-fruit aromas are additionally enhanced by maceration and a spontaneous fermentation. Particular yeasts are required so that these aromas can be set free during fermentation.

ROSE

The smell of roses – which is also found in lychees – is formed in the grape skin by monoterpenes (flavor compounds) and transferred into the must during maceration. The rose-like smell is typical of Rieslings from relatively warm winegrowing regions and vintages or for ripe Spätlese wines from light, permeable, sandy soils.

FRESH GRASS

The smell of a freshly mown meadow is found above all in Rieslings from more northern, and therefore cool wine growing areas, although also in wines from substantial loam soils such as typically appear in Franken, Rheinhessen, in the Pfalz and in Baden. Grassy aromas may also be an indication of unripe grapes, where other aromas have not been sufficiently developed. This aroma can also be caused by short whole-bunch pressing.

RAISINS AND CARAMEL

As soon as Riesling grapes are affected with botrytis, the aforementioned fruit aromas are decomposed step by step, and the formation of raisin-like and caramel-like aromas then occurs. The raisin tone comes about via the botrytis fungus which leads to loss of fluid and at the same time to a concentration of the aromas in the grape. With Beerenauslese, Trockenbeerenauslese and Eiswein, it is in fact difficult to recognize Riesling by its aroma.

AROMAS FROM FERMENTATION

YEAST

Since many Rieslings – like Champagne – are left on the lees for some time to round off the flavor, young Rieslings can be characterized by an intensive smell of fresh baking-yeast. The lees contact intensifies the mouthfeel, and at the same time the Rieslings become softer and smoother. The yeast aroma, however, prevails noticeably at the expense of the delicate fruit aromas. The wines only then really begin to shine after a certain ripening period.

ARCTIC-FRESH CANDY

It may perhaps sound unusual, but shortly after fermentation some Rieslings include a noticeably fresh, cool, almost eucalyptus-like "Arctic-fresh-candy" aroma. Fruity esters, the acetates responsible for this characteristic smell, are formed from alcohol and acids (acetic acid) during fermentation. This special aroma is typical of cool-fermentation and simple wines.

ALCOHOLS

Alcohol is the popular designation for ethanol, which is formed from the grape sugar during fermentation of the grape juice. Along with ethanol, there are other, higher alcohols present in wine, which function as creators of aroma and taste (e.g. glycerol). If simple Rieslings are fermented at too high a temperature, they often exhibit a dull, piercing character, which can be attributed to excessive levels of these higher alcohols.

PINEAPPLE

An especially pleasing ester-component resulting from fermentation can be described as a slightly sweet, fresh-pineapple aroma. This rather short-lived note is fostered by cool fermentation and particular strains of yeast.

All of the aromas mentioned originate directly from fermentation and are distinctly perceptible in the olfactory make-up of a Riesling only in its first year. After one year their intensity significantly falls off. Conversely, the aromas of ripeness increase with age.

AROMAS FROM RIPENING

HONEY

The aroma spectrum of honey ranges from the delicately fruity, sweetish nuances of blossom honeys up to the smoky, stringent notes of acacia honey. The honey characteristic appears above all in Rieslings older than ten years, and it increases noticeably with age, because the other fruit aromas in the "acidic" range of Riesling are reduced. In principle: the higher the grape quality, the more a Riesling will tend to form honey aromas.

ORANGE PEEL

Together with apple, peach and mango fruit aromas, the orange-peel aroma forms the "second spring" of a Riesling, emerging after two to three years of maturation. This prominent aroma trait thereby typically belongs to the ripeness characteristic of a classic Riesling of Spätlese grade or higher, and can last for up to ten years. This olfactory component occurs more often in southern winegrowing regions in Rieslings from fully-ripe grape harvests.

PETROLEUM

The oft-cited note of petroleum or kerosene describes an aroma that is frequently associated with mature Riesling, but more precisely corresponds to the smell of linseed oil. The odor derives from a waste product of the yellow carotenoids (organic pigments, present also in carrots), with which the grape skin protects itself against the stresses of the environment. The risk of a Riesling developing this petroleum note when mature is greater in hotter years and in warmer winegrowing regions. This very prominent flavor phenomenon restricts worldwide Riesling cultivation to the more northern and cooler regions.

WALNUT

The aging of Rieslings is closely associated with oxidation, that is, the reaction of oxygen with the ingredients of the wine. Oxidation products, such as for example aldehydes, have a nutty and slightly bitter flavor, which can extend to an undesirable sherry tone.

TERROIR AND AROMAS

BLUE SLATE
AND
GREEN APPLE

The soils of the more northerly Riesling-growing areas such as the Mosel, Saar, Ruwer, Mittelrhein and the lower Rheingau are above all characterized by slate. This soil is very permeable as a result of its stratified structure and its consequent capacity to store the sun's warmth particularly well. The combination of harsh, stony slate, the storage of warmth and the incredibly long vegetation period is what makes it possible in the first place to produce such outstanding, complex Rieslings with delicate acidity and splendid fruity sweetness. Rieslings from slate soils are typically characterized by a fresh, green, apple note and an accompanying mineral note. This aromatic make-up is attributable to the relatively cool northern location and the lack of a nutrient-rich soil, thereby permitting the fine minerality to be clearly tasted.

RED SHALE
AND
HAYSEED • HERBAL AROMA

This shale gets its red color through the incorporation of iron. The soil type is found for example in the Roter Hang (Rheinhessen), in the Ürziger Würzgarten (Mosel) and in the Birkweiler Kastanienbusch (Pfalz). The Rieslings that grow on these shale soils can smell and taste almost severe and eccentric in their early years, and as a rule they require somewhat more time in order to develop their aromas. The fine nuances of hayseed, light, spicy herbal notes and terse minerality are characteristic of red shale. When such Rieslings from red shale have reached their full quality potential they begin to exhibit very individual and above all impressive personalities.

VARIEGATED SANDSTONE
AND
APRICOT

Alongside slate, variegated sandstone forms the second classic soil type, appearing for example in the southern Pfalz site of Siebeldinger im Sonnenschein, in the entire Mittelhaardt as well as in the vineyards of Forster Kirchenstück (Pfalz), Centgrafenberg (Franken), Durbacher Plauelrain (Baden), Spiegel, Kessler and Kitterlé (Alsace). A weathered soil of variously colored, mostly red, variegated sandstone allows rapid warming and is able to store water only moderately, as a result of its sandy structure. The vines therefore tend to exhibit moderate growth and tolerate a long vegetation period which permits a more intensive formation of aromas. Rieslings from variegated sandstone usually have a fruity, very aromatic character, clearly reminiscent of apricot, and they possess a vigorous body and somewhat milder acidity.

MUSCHELKALK
AND
MANGO

Riesling does not only grow in stony, sparse soils, but can develop its grandeur in heavy, limey soils, such as in the Homburger Kallmuth and Würzburger Stein vineyards (Franken), Flonheimer Feuerberg (Rheinhessen), Kallstadter Saumagen and Königsbacher Idig (Pfalz), Steinklotz, Osterberg and Bruderthal (Alsace). The fertile, nutrient-rich soils with a well-balanced water supply produce Rieslings of a vigorous and opulent style whose acidity, as a rule, does not fully come to the fore and interacts on the whole somewhat more mildly. The exotic, fruity notes, which may be characterized as mango aromas, intensify in the wine with an increase of chalk in the soil. Rieslings from muschelkalk soils nevertheless always require a little more time and a little more ripeness in order to develop to their full grandeur.

TERROIR AND AROMAS

PORPHYRY
AND
MINERALITY

This rock is of volcanic origin and forms the substrate for a soil which is as a rule sparse, with little humus overlay and fine earth, such as is found in the Traiser Bastei and in the Norheimer Kafels (Nahe), in Siefersheimer Heerkretz (Rheinhessen), but also in the Wachau and Kamptal regions. The aerated, water-permeable and easily-warmed soil can produce Rieslings – rather like those from blue-slate soils – with mineral, almost dusty notes, as if it had just rained on a road surface. The combination of a long ripening period, characteristic mineral and fruity aromas, fine acidity and elegant fruit creates a many-facetted Riesling. Porphyry soils, together with slate soils, are perfectly suited to produce splendid, gleaming, fruity-sweet Rieslings of almost unlimited storage potential.

PRIMITIVE ROCKS
AND
QUINCE • SMOKE

Gneiss and granite characterize the primitive-rock soils, which are prevalent above all in the Wachau region. These stony, sparse, easily-warmed but water-permeable soils impart to the Riesling fine quince aromas. For protection, these Rieslings, which are subject to extreme sunshine on the steep terraces, accumulate tannins in their grape skins. During fermentation, the tannins can be rearranged via the yeast, into odor-active, slightly smoky aromas. These aromas, which in other soil formations would typically appear in hot years, decompose within one to two years. Thanks to their ripeness, these weighty Rieslings, grown on primitive rocks, shine forth with an incredible presence and complexity.

LOESS-LOAM
AND
GRAPEFRUIT

This soil structure varies from a purely loess soil on the Kaiserstuhl in Baden through strongly loamy soils such as are found for example in the southern Pfalz region and in Rheinhessen, to pebbly soils in northern Rheinhessen and in Franken. In order to counter the characteristic growth potential of such soils, the winemakers need to reduce the yields to a reasonable amount in good time. Commonly described as heavy, these soils – in contrast to the permeable, stony soils – are able to store sufficient moisture, thanks to their water-storage potential particularly in warmer years (2003), to provide for the grapes. Rieslings from loess-loam soils come across as more enduring and more vigorous, the relative coolness of the soil promoting fine, citrus-like aroma notes reminiscent of grapefruit.

KEUPER
AND
HONEYDEW MELON

Although they are not considered as classic Riesling soils, the heavy, water-retentive, clayey marl soils are nevertheless suitable for Riesling cultivation. The fertile but predominantly difficult-to-warm soils bring forth Rieslings which in their structure tend toward an aroma of ripe honeydew melon and other exotic notes, and present themselves as being rather less spicy, vigorous and opulent. Heavy keuper soils are found in Untertürkheim and Fellbach (Württemberg), in Iphofen (Franken) as well as in Altenberg de Bergbieten (Alsace). What the soil lacks in heat-storage potential must be compensated for by a particularly well exposed site and accordingly high levels of sunshine.

TERROIR

Down to earth

Wine landscapes are cultural landscapes situated on old strata of earth which divulge their history to the wine-drinker in every sip. It is not surprising then, that there is more than one valid definition for the interaction between soil, location, vine and wine, which is commonly termed terroir, or that the definition of what this term means ranges from esoteric nonsense to a valid quality standard.

Terroir: when translated, the French word means nothing more than soil. At the same time, in the dictionary there is the note: "particularly suited to winemaking." On the other hand, the really significant content is not quite so easy to establish, but is nevertheless more than a matter of purely layers of earth. So what then is really concealed behind this word, what is really hidden in the term terroir?

TERROIR, SCIENTIFICALLY

What we can smell and taste in wine is the result of various factors which are generally designated as terroir. For science, the sensory aspects of a wine stand in direct relationship with certain measurable quantities which, combined, determine the influence of the terroir. Here, it is not solely a matter of the nutrient content or the water-storage capacity of a soil. The scientific approach includes the topography – the slope gradient or the geographical alignment of a vineyard – and the relevant microclimate. Sites shielded by a mountain range protect Rieslings from incident cold air. In sites open to winds there is the risk that warm air could be swept away. Sites at the foot of river valleys are often sub-

Winemaking as a geographical challenge, here
for example on the steep Pündericher Marienlay
vineyard at the Mosel

ject to autumnal fog, and are therefore more likely to be subject to formations of botrytis, which likewise influences the terroir-characteristic of the wine. Where Riesling is situated in shady and cool valleys, the terroir is unable to mature because of the lack of grape ripeness. Even the color of the soil plays a role, since darker soils warm up more rapidly than light-colored soils. It is scientifically contested as to how far the human factor – beginning with the choice of grape variety, right up to the decisions to be made in the cellar – is a part of the terroir-concept.

TERROIR, PHILOSOPHICALLY

The philosophical approach is not limited just to the various soil structures, but stretches past the measurable dimension of the terroir and beyond. Terroir is accordingly an interconnected biological network, which literally forms the foundation of nature. It is the lifegiving reservoir for the vine, from which it develops its growth and is thereby a crucial element in the quality of the wine.

There is however one further aspect: What would wine be without the people, the region and the culture and history bound up with it? What role does man play in the system? This notion of the terroir-concept therefore comprises – along with environmental and biological factors – ultimately the human influences such as technology, vinification, cellar management, and also history and economics. The choice of grape variety may well be a politically motivated factor or a choice determined by historical-cultural points of view.

WINE: THE MOUTHPIECE

The terroir by itself cannot communicate with us. Without grapes, without wine, the terroir

Reinhard Löwenstein has his own idea of terroir

remains "speechless". The vine is needed to make the various factors of the birthplace of the wine transparent in terms of flavor, that is, to make a certain typicity recognizable. This means: what grows here, has typical and thereby recognizable characteristics. Where the soil in which the Riesling grows is characterized by slate, then this note will be discernible once again in the wine itself and will characterize it. This traceability of flavor is present above all in high-quality wines, where the

THE VINEYARD AS A SYSTEM

"The term terroir describes the comprehensive and complex 'vineyard as system': great, individual wines ripen here in a constructive interplay between soil, climate, variety and winemaker. They form the antithesis of the oft technically outstanding Coca-Cola-wines with a flavor somewhere between 'boring' and 'soulless monster' which today, as globalization proceeds, are conquering the world's markets. Terroir wines belong to the world of culture. They are beyond scientific comprehension or even objective evaluation. On the contrary: they are subtle and full of finesse, incalculable, mutable, scrutinizing, provocative, calling everything into question and thus allowing an emancipatory journey into the exciting world of authentic flavor."

Reinhard Löwenstein,
winemaker, Winningen, Mosel

vinification is adjusted to the individual conditions of the terroir. In the same way the provenance of a simple Riesling – whether from the Mosel or the Pfalz – can easily be determined. The higher the grape quality, the more exactly can we distinguish even narrowly defined terroirs, which are situated perhaps only 500 yards apart. Hardly anywhere in the world is there a variety that so sensitively reacts and reveals such a strongly recognizable typicity as Riesling does. However, where high yields, extensive winemaking and over-enthusiastic cellar management come together, then all forms of terroir-concept, and often even the recognition of the Riesling variety, become impossible.

TRUST IS GOOD

Using the potentials of soil, site and climate, the winemaker must weigh up and decide which variety would best express and most authentically characterize these natural requirements of the wine. In this respect, terroir also denotes knowledge of, and confidence in the familiar soil and in the natural surroundings. From the constellation of soil, climate, variety and winemaker, the unmistakable character of a wine evolves through harmonious interaction.

There is still some disagreement as to which minerals and which individual components of the soil primarily and durably define the sensory characteristics of wines. The view is held that the most full-bodied, richest wines grow in lime-rich soils, as for example with those found in Tuscany, Burgundy, Bordeaux and Rioja. This terroir concept does not entirely hold true for Riesling, since some great Rieslings grow in such varying soils as slate, variegated sandstone, muschelkalk and in primitive rocks. Riesling creates a furore precisely because it can produce impressive qualities in non-classic terroirs, such as in powerful loess soils.

CONTROL IS BETTER

What happens then, when man manipulates the terroir – for example through irrigation, which would probably not take place naturally? Water supply is a risk factor particularly in dry years, which in insufficiently supplied locations can lead to a significant delay in the ripening of the grapes.

In some Riesling regions – for instance in Wachau or the New World – the irrigation of vineyards has long since become standard. In Germany, larger vine areas were irrigated for the first time during the hot 2003 vintage.

"Each vineyard is at the same time the boundary of a wine, each individual terroir represents another world, in which the variety does not necessarily need to be recognizable. This is why in France the point of origin of the wine is declared. The vineyard is like a personality, an individual with its own language. Terroir is a style that you do not have to like, but you can recognize it straightaway. The energy of the terroir is in the grape, and the winemaker needs to recognize to which variety the terroir is best suited, with which wines the site could best interact. A single grape variety on its own brings too little differentiation into the terroir's language, similarly, one cannot explain the world on one sheet of paper and with only one word. Terroir is the idea of "being one", in the way that all colors together make the picture. The terroir and the vines must interact in the same way as nose and mouth in taste."

Jean-Michel Deiss,
winemaker, Bergheim, Alsace

By means of analytical tests in the Rheingau Riesling vineyards, Prof. Hans Schultz of the Geisenheim research institute was able to determine that particularly in the top-quality sites, where increased warming in future will lead more frequently to a no-longer acceptable water shortage, that specific use of irrigation is more likely to promote the terroir.

For, acute water shortage in Riesling can lead to an excessive build-up of tannic acids, insufficient acidity and undesired aromas, and also to a reduction in the storage potential of the wine.

TERROIR WINE, A SYNTHESIS OF THE ARTS

In this way, the winemaker can have a decisive influence on the grape quality, through irrigation, tillage, plant protection, regulation of yield, maintenance of the grapes' health and a late picking. If it were possible for ten winemakers to produce in the same vineyard, the result would be ten quite different wines. Ultimately, the production of great wines is a matter of perceptive flair and instinct. The intensity of human activity in the vineyard and during vinification determines the extent to which the character of a terroir can be brought out. Committed winemakers are able harmoniously and appropriately to incorporate the mineral content of their vineyard soils into their Rieslings and to capture the aromas and the spices of vigorous soils in their wines. Excessive yields, inordinate botrytis, an excessive interference through cellar management, but also inexperience in handling the terroir can obstruct the development of the flavor potential of a site. Whether – as some winemakers argue – the introduction of cultured yeasts produces in the terroir a more authentic appearance than spontaneous yeasts, remains a stimulating discussion. Ultimately, terroir is what gives the wine its entirely individual, characteristic local note, beyond all international fashions and trends, which are the enemy of all regional individuality.

CHAPTER 4

RIESLING, A MATTER OF TASTE

RIESLING PERSONALITIES WITH STYLE

A SOUND BASIS

Inexpensive wines for every day

Even now, in many countries, wine has the status of a food, which is integrated into the respective social environment with its culinary culture, and thus represents a basic, everyday product. Wine is not therefore, an exception, but may rather be considered – in moderation – as the rule. A reasonable level of quality, allowing the daily enjoyment of wine, is therefore desirable, both with regard to health aspects, as well as affordability. A standard dictionary would define "basis" as "the foundation upon which something can be supported and upon which it can develop." Rieslings, which offer a simple but recommendable drinking experience, are available from all German winegrowing areas, since they form the economic foundation for many estates, cellars and wine growers' cooperatives. This fact should always be borne in mind even when the evaluations in the wine guides and magazines concentrate much more on the relatively small amounts of top-quality wines which are produced. Wines in large amounts or in bulk are still produced in the lower price categories, because wines are first and foremost commodities and thus an important economic factor. Basic wines, which can be produced in large amounts, therefore represent the lion's share in all wine regions. That the quality diverges wildly and that wines are offered which are not always to be recommended, unfortunately damages the reputation of Riesling.

BULK VERSUS QUALITY

There are some supermarkets and discounters in which Riesling is already being offered from €1.50 per bottle. If one deducts the costs for bottle, cork, label, labor and transport, there remains just a minimum (hardly more than ten cents) for the contents, and it should be quite clear to anyone that reasonable quality in such cases cannot even be considered. The battered image of cooperatives and cellars, producing only cheap, bulk goods, is therefore certainly in some cases justified. Particularly the German wine industry still suffers from the "Kellergeister" syndrome: that cheap, sparkling wine-beverage, by which, since the mid-1970's, the reputation of German Riesling has been constantly battered.

THERE IS A DIFFERENT WAY

Nevertheless, the size of a business or its economic structure is not necessarily an indication of cheap, bulk products. Indeed, modern production methods in the vineyard and in the cellar facilitate attractive Riesling qualities being brought onto the market on a large scale. Many cellars and wine-growing cooperatives primarily produce wines for everyday consumption in this way. They offer spotless quality at a relatively low price without the pretension of an elaborate Riesling specialty individually crafted by hand.

The use of cultured yeasts has a no less important role here than the option of cool, controlled fermentation. The influential fresh wind from the new world of wine is reflected in the new quality concepts from cellars such as Reh-Kendermann, Peter Mertes and Zimmermann-Graeff & Müller with their Riesling steep-site concept.

The other side of the coin is however that wine production conceived for a specific bulk unfortunately conceals the danger of a faceless standardization of wine production. The end result is Rieslings without individuality that betray all the flavoral aspects of the variety, including their fruity taste, but nothing of their place of origin.

In contrast, many winemakers offer sound, basic qualities as Guts-Rieslinge (estate Rieslings), which at least carry the signature of an estate and of a region. As a rule, these wines are a good and informative introduction to the entire product range.

ALL-ROUNDERS FOR EVERY DAY ENJOYMENT

This usually uncomplicated, simple type should offer sound quality at a reasonable price. They are found on the market with such designations as: estate wine, everyday wine, goblet or bread-and-butter-Riesling. They are likewise to be found in well-organized wine stores as well as directly from the winemaker and sometimes are even to be found on the wine-shelves at the supermarket. These wines, which are on offer from dry to fruity-sweet, make no demands on cellar space: they are produced for immediate consumption and may by all means be stored for a few days along with all the other groceries in the fridge – well cooled, ready-to-drink or else as wine for cooking.

Boris Kranz from the southern Pfalz comes from a classic family business

In point of taste, sound basic Rieslings exhibit above all the typicity of the variety, without suggesting the terroir or any possible variations introduced in the winemaking process. They lay no claim to any multilayered quality, nor to depth, let alone complexity. They are Rieslings which, as a rule, are bottled without a site designation. Above all, the flavor is marked by a simple but convincing fresh Riesling aroma, which arises from a balanced ratio of fruit, alcohol, acidity and sweetness.

Boris Kranz
WEINGUT FAMILIE KRANZ

The Kranz estate in Ilbesheim is a close-knit community in the best sense of the word. Boris Kranz is responsible for the vineyard and the cellar, his father, Robert, looks after deliveries and occasionally the distilling of schnaps. His mother Lilo has on-site sales as her main task, and Boris' wife, Kerstin, is responsible for trade sales and marketing. "We are a real family business," says mother Lilo Kranz, and all agree. They are happy to be a family business and keep the way clear for their "winemaker Boris" so that he can concentrate on his wines. Boris Kranz makes good Rieslings, sound qualities at reasonable prices:

"The simple Riesling liter-wine makes up a good tenth of our entire production. Our customers expect consistent quality at a high level, every year! Quality is the thread that runs unbroken throughout our entire product range. I make sure of this with the fresh, discreetly fruity liter-wines in just the same way as with the high-value growths."

The label displays a large number and a tiny monkey. "In the southern Pfalz every small community has a nickname, we are the Ilbesheim monkeys," explains Kranz. In addition, the young winemaker has founded the "Südpfalz-Connection" with five of his friends: "The collaboration is proving to be distinctly positive, because we are not only friends, but we also exchange professional experiences, we taste together, express criticism in a positive

sense, and as often as possible embark on wine-exploration expeditions." A close-knit group of friends, all with the same ambition: enjoying life with good wine.

Klaus R. Scherner
WEINGUT SCHERNER-KLEINHANSS

Klaus R. is a representative of the ninth generation to have practiced winemaking in Flörsheim-Dalsheim. "Family tradition as a passion," says Scherner, "and *with* passion. However, that developed only after some years." Scherner did not really wish to be-

The much traveled Rheinhessian Klaus R. Scherner is a dedicated advocate of German Riesling

come a winemaker. "After high-school graduation, I enrolled to study musicology in Mainz. Although things turned out quite differently: In southern France I had something like a key oenophile experience, I returned to Germany and promptly began to study winemaking at Geisenheim technical college." Scherner wrote his final-year thesis at the institute for vine breeding. "I then wanted to get to know the world of wine, went to Canada for some years and subsequently to Brazil." At some point he returned to Flörsheim-Dalsheim in Rheinhessen, and he took over the estate from his parents. "Riesling is not our main variety, we also traditionally cultivate Pinot varieties and Silvaner. Although Riesling is my great love," says Klaus R.

Scherner. He mainly produces dry wines. With low yields, selective hand-picking and sensitive vinification, he lives up to the quality yardstick he has set himself – and this includes the so-called simple wines. *"Quality must be an uninterrupted constant. Where there is no solid foundation, the tip of the spire will tremble. Simple Rieslings particularly must be good, so that without any great tasting affectations, the daily pleasure of drinking is not spoiled. I therefore like to offer sound, basic qualities at a reasonable price alongside the higher Prädikat wines."*

Sebastian Schäfer
Weingut Joh. Bapt. Schäfer

"I attempt to produce wines which I am happy to drink myself. Wines with character, real individualists!" That's what the price-list from Sebastian Schäfer says. He took over the six-hectare family business in 2001 and has devoted himself entirely to the craft of winemaking. "Wine is everything for me, wine is my hobby, my life!" One could confidently replace the word 'wine' with 'Riesling.' Sebastian Schäfer is full of energy and ambition, and he loves Riesling. He would prefer to go right to the top, straightaway, to the place where the Riesling-elite of the Nahe is to be found. The young winemaker is heading in the right direction, and one should keep him in view. Schäfer's collection exhibits his unconditional qualitative demands upon himself and his wines. Since his entry into his parents' business, he has been annually producing a

Sebastian Schäfer will continue to be a source of surprises in the world of Riesling

very presentable Riesling Classic: quite clearly structured and superbly delicious. In addition the Classic is not very expensive but is an ideal introduction to the world of Riesling. It has only one message and that is: simply good. If all Classic Rieslings had such a quality-oriented background, this wine concept would establish itself more effectively in Germany and make many things simpler. For those who make a good start will also achieve their aims. For Sebastian Schäfer, things are looking good.

Jochen Dreissigacker
WEINGUT FRIEDER DREISSIGACKER

Much is happening in the Bechtheim family business, and one can rest assured that the estate will develop well in the coming years. The conditions are good, and at the heart of the business is a dedicated family: father, mother and their two sons, Christian and Jochen: "My parents created a wine estate from the former, classic, mixed-agricultural operation, switched from sales by-the-barrel to bottles, installed guest rooms and, at some point, opened the "Strausswirtschaft" (traditionally, a winemaker's cottage for wine tasting guests). We all have a specific task in our family and the business runs like clockwork," says Jochen Dreissigacker, who had initially sought his professional fortune in the world of figures. However, after a thorough, basic training in the revenue service, he was bitten by the wine bug. He turned his back on the tax office and became a winemaker in his parents'

business. His brother Christian is responsible for the cellars of the estate. Their mother, Ute, is rightly proud of this form of family conflation with a professional background to it: "Our whole life is wine," she says. From May through June, she is in charge of the estate's own "Strausswirtschaft", and her sons deliver the wines for it: "We require a sound Riesling for our rustic cuisine, a proverbial bread-and-butter Riesling which our guests love and of course preferably drink by the bottle, because it simply tastes good and is inexpensive." This is certainly only the beginning, since Jochen Dreissigacker and his family have more potential, of course in respect of Riesling.

Cave Vinicole de Ribeauvillé

This tiny town in the heart of Alsace is much loved by tourists, above all because of its picturesque historic heart. Only a few people know that the oldest winegrowers' cooperative in France is located only a stone's throw distant from the main street. This stately, yellow building however, can hardly be overlooked, and the wines on offer are, quite simply, commendable.

In the enormous vinotheque, all wines from those growers affiliated to the cooperative can be tasted, an extremely interesting flavoral stroll through the numerous varieties and soil structures of Alsace. After all, the sunlit hills all around Ribeauvillé are considered some of the best vine slopes in the region. Cave Vinicole de Ribeauvillé itself cultivates ten grand-cru sites and is well known far and wide for its sound quality. Equally, the cooperative scores as many points in the wine guides as other distinguished estates.

Riesling plays an important role among the wines on offer, and along with the simple Cuvée Prestige it is also produced and offered under its individual site names. The Riesling collection "Lieuts-Dits" consists of wines from various terroirs such as for instance Steinacker, Pflänzer, Mühlforst and Silberberg. The refreshingly dry and fruity Rieslings display vigor and body with a crisp acidity, and they appear in the next-higher quality level, "L'or du terroir" to be even finer and more polished. Rieslings for everyday enjoyment, suitable for simple, rustic cuisine.

Jürgen Hofmann
REH-KENDERMANN

In Germany, the word "Weinkellerei" (winery, processing bought-in grape juice) smacks of staleness. Again and again, wineries are presented as scapegoats, because they have allegedly damaged the image of German wines abroad with "Liebfraumilch" and with dumping prices. This is true, but not always. Indeed, the size of a business does not in itself inevitably mean lower wine quality, or vice versa. Reh-Kendermann in Bingen is one of the most modern wineries in the country and the leading exporter of German wines. The company is under the private ownership of Carl and Andrea Reh, and it produces over 70 million bottles of wine annually, and a good 10% of this is Riesling. For the production of brand-name wines, grapes are bought via long-term cultivation contracts. "Our team manages the work in the vineyard, selects the right moment for harvesting and controls the

subsequent fermentation. In spite of the size of the business, we continue our unflinchingly high regard for quality, otherwise our wine concepts do not pay off," says head winemaker Jürgen Hofmann. Reh-Kendermann has set a further qualitative focus in its own business with the terroir concept, which was implemented for the first time in 2002.

"Meanwhile, we have our own vineyards on the Mosel, in the Pfalz and in Rheinhessen. This enables us to vinify Rieslings with their respective individual terroir character in each case. The Mosel represents slate and minerality. In the Pfalz, Riesling in limey soils is likely to produce exotic fruit aromas, and in Rheinhessen, in particular in the Roter Hang, it manifests, on red shale, more herbal, spicy notes. All three wines were cool-fermented with the same yeasts in steel tanks."

The result is three completely differing Rieslings that, in terms of flavor, quite distinctly exhibit the regionally typical variations. However, Jürgen Hofmann is not yet content with what has been achieved.

"In the course of time we have got to know our vineyards much better and we can now act on the quality more individually. We no longer cut out bunches so early but instead break off some shoots for yield-reduction purposes. This year, for the first time I have fermented some batches with wild yeasts and then blended them together, which noticeably gave the wines more substance."

An he sticks to his guns: "My dream is of oak barrels, which would help me to introduce a bit more substance into the Rieslings through their effects on the wines."

Tenders are already lying on his desk.

Sister Andrea and Sister Thekla

St Hildegard Convent estate

There is not much that remains of the active, monastic winemaking culture. Most abbeys have become secularized or now have a different use. In the Rheingau, whose wine history has been characterized for centuries by the powerful Cistercian abbey of Eberbach and the Benedictine monastery on the Johannisberg, this tradition is still maintained by Benedictine nuns.

The activities of the order with regard to winemaking stretch back to the time of the founding abbess, the St Hildegard of Bingen. Today, the convent estate is managed by Sisters Andrea and Thekla, and both have graduated in winemaking studies. It was only in the convent that these Benedictine nuns were initially introduced to working in the vineyard and, as they admit, also to the drinking of wine. Traditions must be maintained. About 6½ hectares of vines – primarily in Rüdesheim sites right around the convent – are cultivated by the women of the order together with master-of-wine Arnuf Steinheimer, and more than 80% of the total area is planted with Riesling. With clerical approbation, the naturally pure wines are licensed for use as communion wine, As before, all wines of the convent are subject to the basic principle that "the matter may not be altered." Naturally, the wines are also suitable for daily use, the convent estate offers good Riesling qualities in all flavoral varieties in its smart convent shop.

Rolf Münster

Winzergenossenschaft Mayschoss

On the steep, slate slopes of the Ahr valley, Riesling vines are rather seldom to be found, since the winegrowers receive more money for their red grapes. However, rarities have their lure, and that's why Rolf Münster – since 1988, the head winemaker of the Mayschoss winegrowers' cooperative – has this noble variety especially close to his heart. Of the approximately 36 hectares which Riesling takes up along the Ahr, the co-operative is responsible for over half. Riesling vines are found above all in particularly dry, stony locations, while Spätburgunder (Pinot Noir), when it grows on slate, requires a somewhat deeper layer, so that a consistent water supply can be assured.

"Pure slate is no problem for Riesling, it simply burrows a way through with its root structure, in order to reach sufficient supplies of nutrients and minerals. Some of the vines are 100 years old and are still root-genuine, non-grafted cuttings, and they produce very small, loose-bunched, aromatic grapes. The best conditions for Riesling and the correspondingly most suitable sites with a good proportion of fine slate are found upstream from Rech along the Ahr. The soils along the lower Ahr are too deep as a rule to produce discreetly fruity, elegant Rieslings with substance."

Around 70% of the Mayschoss Rieslings appear in the basic wine sector, and the remaining 30% are developed according to quality and must weight into Spätlese and Auslese wines with the site designations of Mayschosser Laacherberg or Mayschosser Mönchberg. Among the favorites of the cooperative members are their excellent, multifaceted ice wines.

DELICATE FINESSE

Light flavorsome Kabinetts

Riesling is no delicate little plant, it is a robust vine which prefers cool, moderate weather, rather than warmer, sunnier climes. Indeed, only in such moderate climates is the variety able to produce light, lacy wines, which are still substantial and expressive in their flavor. The Rieslings of this category are like a fleeting touch that addresses the sensibility of all the senses. Delicate Rieslings chime with soft tones and push the discreet, subtle aspects of the variety to the fore. They present a fine overall taste to the palate, like a silken ribbon, dancing almost weightlessly, like a melody in the wind, spiraling around itself.

Delicate Rieslings emerge unobtrusively and graciously, but that does not mean they have no flavor. They reveal their forte at relatively low alcohol contents with a balanced structure that neatly sets accents, without rising above a certain intensity. They are graceful wines, which justify themselves without any effusive opulence, they are balanced wines that, in their elegant lightness, have something almost insouciant. This delicate finesse is accompanied by a minerality that does not seem to exhibit any heavy, earthy notes, but reveals, rather, finely chiseled mineral nuances, which ideally combine with the fruit aromas and add to a multifaceted overall taste.

It is the archetypal Kabinett wine from slate-rich vineyards, such as have a long tradition along the Mosel, Saar, Ruwer, Mittelrhein, Nahe and in the Rheingau. Kabinett wines, which are below Spätlese wines in ranking order, thanks to their low alcohol content (7.5 to 10.5% vol.), represent above all a unique category of naturally light wines. The Wachau wine category Steinfeder also embraces this type, with its magnificent light, aromatic Rieslings, which are allowed to have no more than 11% vol. alcohol.

Only in northerly and cool winegrowing areas can such wines emerge, which even without the intensity of the alcohol as flavor-carrier unite a multilayered fruit aroma and finesse with an intensive flavor. They are – if you will – a legally determined wine type, and in the international world of wine virtually without competition. In addition, this style of wine can considerably improve in format via a hint of sweetness which harmoniously integrates and rounds off the acidity. These particularly special Kabinetts offer easy-drinking pleasure with delicate finesse and a playful acidity.

Stefan Breuer
WEINGUT ALTENKIRCH

"Wine should rather be captured in the glass, not in words," says Stefan Breuer. "In any case, there is no ultimate flavor-solution; precisely Riesling, with its unique diversity, continues to be somewhat of an individual."
Breuer's vineyards lie at the western tip of the Rheingau: a few yards further, and we're in the Mittelrhein.
"A lot of slate and quartzite, and also some limey loess-loam. The vineyard injects a powerful shot of minerality into the Riesling. The terroir must prevail, it is our potential and capital. To listen in to the soil, to understand it, to interpret its signs: in a certain respect, winemakers are the servants of their soils and the assistant of the grape variety, which is there to interpret the soil. I am looking for this typicity, the original, non-derivative type, which the soil seeks to acquaint me with. This is why my Rieslings are lean, almost tender, and at the same time refreshing, fruity and accompanied by a fine but aromatic acidity and distinctive minerality. One glass from these Rieslings does not quite satisfy one's appetite, but intensifies the desire for a second."

Matthias Müller
WEINGUT MATTHIAS MÜLLER

The narrow valley with the high, steep rock faces along the Mittelrhein projects a romantic and perhaps a somewhat dreamy picture. But appearances are deceptive. Along the 75 miles from Bingen to Bonn, one sees not only pretty, timber-framed houses and enchanting castles. There are also winemakers committed to the preservation of this unique wine landscape. One of them is Matthias Müller in Spay. He cultivates eight hectares in the Bopparder Hamm, which, with 85 hectares, is the largest contiguous site in the Mittelrhein region. Matthias Müller has for a few years worked increasingly with the vineyard's own wild yeasts:
"Riesling, developed only with cultured yeasts, always runs the risk of tasting regular and uniform. My wines should reflect the fine mineral taste of slate and the typicity of the Mittelrhein. It need not always be a Spätlese, particularly Kabinett wines possess the light interplay of acidity, fruit and minerality."

Stefan Breuer is a Riesling protagonist at the western tip of the Rheingau region

However, Herr Müller also agrees that there is less and less commitment on the part of the winemakers in this wine category.

"In a direct comparison with the entire selection of wines, Kabinett wines are losing more and more ground with the consumer. A light Kabinett wine does not have an easy time of it against the more mature and correspondingly more supple Spätlese wines. Too bad that the Kabinett category appears to be a dying species along the Mittelrhein. At the same time, Kabinett wines can be great accompaniments to food, since they have all the characteristics of what a wine needs, without upstaging the lead player."

Hopefully, Matthias Müller will dedicate himself to his Kabinett wines for some time to come!

Theo Haart
Weingut Reinhold Haart

"Unfortunately, Kabinett is an almost forgotten story. In former times, under the name of Kabinett, winemakers bottled a light wine with low alcohol, tender fruit and fine, mineral notes. Today, thanks to general yield reductions, the wines are more vigorous, more complex and thus also have higher alcohol levels."

Theo Haart is one of the quieter members of the wine community, and his Spätlese and Auslese wines are well-known far and wide, but he goes into passionate raptures in favor of Kabinett wines.

"Kabinett Rieslings in the residual-sweet range require minerality as well as a corresponding complexity, in order to soften the sweetness, since they would otherwise swiftly end up in the Spätlese sector. In the Mosel region in the 1970s Kabinett Rieslings were located at just under 80° Oechsle,

Theo Haart's Kabinett Rieslings are among the best wines of the Mosel

which we would today more likely describe as rather thin and meager. As a result of climate change and yield reductions, up to 85° Oechsle is currently considered quite normal, and a Kabinett still tastes like a Kabinett regardless. However, there were, and still are, frequent endeavors to do away with the Kabinett category. This is too bad, since these tenderly interwoven, delicate Rieslings deserve consideration alongside other great wines. We must learn to differentiate between a corpulent and a lacy Riesling. The desirable goal is a shared style."

His son Johannes, after his studies in Geisenheim, will experience Riesling in Australia, in order to then actively come to the aid of his father in the Piesport and Wintrich sites.

Annegret Reh-Gartner

WEINGUT
REICHSGRAF VON KESSELSTATT

She chats pleasantly and charmingly about her wines, always committed and competent, but also critical and searching. Annegret Reh-Gartner has a personality of the sort that one can immediately accept. Despite all the commercial activities which the wine business brings with it, her husband Gerhard Gartner takes care that reassuring tranquility always returns. While the excellent cook presides over the kitchen cabinet, Annegret Reh-Gartner goes into raptures about delicate Kabinett wines: "Riesling is very popular, above all the lighter Kabinett wines are more than ever in demand. We Moselians have a feel for delicate tones." And who could disagree? "What is very important is the typicity of the Rieslings, and on the Mosel they are not bone dry. A touch of residual sweetness even goes well with food." Her husband does not disagree, but only answers approvingly with a nod of his head. In terms of culinary delicacies, no one shows the "old hand" how to do anything anyway.

"This beguiling lightness of Mosel Rieslings distinctly grows in stature and charm thanks to the wines' residual sugar. When the balance of acidity and sweetness is achieved, then the fruit of the Rieslings presents itself in shining clarity. The whole world produces dry wines, and that's how it should be. However, we have here in the Mosel region the best conditions to impart a fine fruit-sweetness to Riesling and at the same time, to convey it playfully, lightly, to the tongue."

Annegret Reh-Gartner thus offers a whole series of aromatic samples from the best sites on the Mosel, Saar and Ruwer.

Clemens Busch
WEINGUT CLEMENS BUSCH

He first made his own Riesling wine about 30 years ago. At that time he did not yet really wish to take over his parents' estate. There was still so much of the world to see and dis-

For Annegret Reh-Gartner Riesling may certainly possess a little residual sweetness

Clemens Busch had already decided on organic wine-making quite some years ago

cover, and so much to learn. However, family circumstances allowed only one decision, and the young Clemens Busch joined the family business at 17 and had to begin right away and in earnest. He would do the same thing again today, he has no doubt about that. Indeed Clemens Busch loves this contact with nature, as does his wife Rita, who runs the estate together with him. From conviction, they live environmentally-conscious lives and have geared their estate entirely to Riesling: "We ourselves are only too happy to drink Riesling to be able to do anything else, and along the

Mosel only Riesling is really suitable anyway!" From their 17th-century timber-framed house on the Mosel at Pünderich, Rita and Clemens Busch can look up directly to their vineyard; steep slopes on the Pündericher Marienburg site, facing south and in a very enclosed space. The Riesling vines are located here in old lots in sparse, stony soils, interspersed with gray and blue slate and red shale. This combination is seldom found. "The rocky terrace is our favorite little vineyard, and it was with this site that the terroir concept became established in our minds. Small, bluff, 75-year-old vines with their roots in gray slate, and botrytis is almost non-existent. A golden opportunity for dry, top-quality wines." Generally, Clemens Busch vinifies about two-thirds of his Rieslings as dry wines.

"The dry Kabinett is a classic wine that enjoys unlimited demand from our customers, and this should remain so. Such a wine has a remarkable amount of flavor and corresponding finesse, and remains nevertheless the lightest wine in the world. In order to achieve this, one requires patience with nature, so that only really ripe grapes are selected. Above all we don't always wish to intervene, we monitor the wines and let them make their own decisions. We cannot achieve every flavor, and we don't wish to."

Anyone wanting to get to know Busch's Riesling personalities should set out for Pünderich.

Rowald Hepp
WEINGUT SCHLOSS VOLLRADS

This is how one imagines a real château at the center of a wine estate: away from the town in a tranquil, natural setting, embedded in a soft landscape of vines. Schloss Vollrads offers impressive insights and outlooks, a place steeped in history, which has been linked to Riesling for centuries, in all its facets and qualities. "The Kabinett wines are our flagship," says Rowald Hepp, who has been running this traditional business since mid-1999.

"The term Kabinettwein appeared as early as 1728 in the annals of the château and for the first time expressed a tastable quality. To this day, the profile of the Kabinett wine is clearly outlined, and one can very clearly taste what a Kabinett wine should represent: not a light wine, but a light Riesling, whose main statement is not due to its alco- *hol. On the contrary! Lower alcohol, but full flavor all the same! All done without botrytis, so that the tender elegance and the richness of nuances are not disguised. In addition, the synergy between the terroir and the variety, which is expressed in a clearly tastable minerality. That is Kabinett."*

Rowald Hepp could go one or two years without Spätlese wines, but not without his Kabinett wines. "Kabinett wines exhibit the profile, the focal point and the expertise of an estate. Nothing can be disguised behind the lightness of these lacy Rieslings, they are absolutely honest wines."

At present, he sees the greatest dynamism in the fruity range, residual-sweet Kabinett Rieslings are in demand as never before. "The fine residual sugar supports the playful character of these wines, although the fruit should not be allowed to push itself to the fore. The minerality is an important flavoral element, which specifically demonstrates the potential and the ability of a Riesling to clearly indicate its home."

Johann Schmelz
WEINGUT SCHMELZ

"Our vineyards are spread over four miles all around Joching, that makes our work no easier, but one gets about in the region," says Johann Schmelz with a hearty laugh. "This means of course differing soils and a very differentiated microclimate. Looking at it this way, our estate lives from diversity." All things are relative.

For Rowald Hepp, the Kabinett Riesling is the flagship of the historic château estate Schloss Vollrads

Johann Schmelz puts his heart and soul into winemaking, and this naturally rubs off. His wife Monika and their two sons, Thomas and Florian, also work on the estate, a real family business. "There is always the question: how can the variety represent the Wachau wine region and the winemakers connected with it? This is my challenge," says Johann Schmelz. And he masters it not only with his creamy Smaragd Rieslings. The lighter, more tender Federspiel wines exhibit fruit, finesse and minerality, and they shine with a quite lacy acidity structure. "The flavoral opulence suffers in no way from their lightness. On the contrary! Riesling can play out its flexibility here: that refreshing, dance-like element, without introducing a high alcohol content into the wine," says the winegrower.

Of course, many Wachau winemakers are focusing their production more and more on the Smaragd qualities. However, it would be a shame if this chance for light, racy and finesse-rich Federspiel wines were eclipsed in the process. So, carry on please, Johann Schmelz!

Reiner Flick
WEINGUT JOACHIM FLICK

Anyone who visited the mill house in Wicker about ten years ago would have found nothing but run-down buildings and builders' rubble, and in the center of the enormous construction site, a young winemaker who, full of vigor, was realizing the idea of his own estate with determination. Today, the mill-house shines with a new brilliance. Reiner and Kirsten Flick have worked hard for just this. The young winemaking couple have turned their business into one of the best wine addresses of the Rheingau. With Riesling of course. "This little wine location always stood in Hochheim's shadow. Wicker was unknown terrain and thus also an unknown terroir." Meanwhile, the world of wine knows Wicker Rieslings, Reiner Flick is something like a local pioneer. "The potential of Wicker sites was quite clear to me, and it was, and still is, a challenge to demonstrate with discernment the possibilities of the terroir above all with Riesling." Reiner Flick extracts his dry Kabinett Rieslings from the stony Wicker soils. Lacy, elegant wines which have a light and tangy effect, but nevertheless display a presence of acidity:

"They are not buttery-soft wines, but real classic Rieslings. Although the wines are tender and light, they are full of substance, forgiving not even the slightest fault. The almost fairy-like lightness can hide nothing behind alcohol, heavy sweetness or a weighty body. Kabinett of this laciness is unique among white wines and presents itself in all its true honesty. Particularly as a result of their tenderness – which nevertheless contains much flavor – these wines are especially stimulating and never dull. In point of fact, Kabinett is an ideal model for Riesling, one in which the grape can act out so much of its elegance and finely-layered quality. It would be a shame if this wine type were squeezed out between the simple wines and the higher-graded Spätlese."

FRUITY DIVERSITY

One of the finest aspects of Riesling

Riesling is an expressive variety, which ideally conveys not only the terroir, but also the aroma and flavor of the grapes. The aromatic potential hidden in these little Riesling grapes is impressive. It can ultimately develop into an astounding fruitiness in the wine.

Apple, lemon, apricot, peach, blossom and mango are only the most obvious and most easily recognizable fruit aromas which Riesling has to offer. The balanced relationship and interplay of these aromas, combined with delicate acidity and low alcohol content, characterize the flavor of these many-layered, fruity Rieslings. They never come across as heavy and filling, they are, rather, tender, playful, delicately fruity and literally seduce you into taking another sip. When Riesling exhibits such a boundless diversity in its fruit structure, then the aromas – embedded in a fine, discreet residual sweetness – taste juicy and delicate, and they give the wine fullness and depth. It is like a feisty bite into a ripe but fresh fruit, whose juice stoutly, yet with a tangy character, fills the palate with a light, pleasant sweetness.

Fruity, multifaceted Rieslings are light in body and alcohol, but possess an overpowering fullness of aromatic and mineral substances. At best, they are like an explosion of flavors and combine concentrated delicately fruity, wonderfully expressed fruit aromas with a subtle, shining acidity and the mineral components of the slaty soil. They virtually dance across the tongue and present a clear freshness to the palate.

In Germany, this conservative Riesling style has survived all trends and fashions from the industrially produced brand wines and the sweet, cloying, cheap Spätlese wines, to the cult of dry wines with excessive acidity, and today it forms one of the foundations of the Riesling renaissance all around the world.

Winemakers such as Joh. Jos. Prüm, Wilhelm Haag, Ernst Loosen and Reinhold Haart in the Mosel region, Egon Müller on the Saar, Maximin Grünhaus on the Ruwer and Helmut Dönnhoff from the Nahe have characterized this wine type with their delicately fruity, nuance-rich Spätlese wines and have set standards. Rieslings with little alcohol, which in spite of their tender structure exhibit the delicate elegance and interplay of fruit-sweetness and acidity which make Riesling so immensely fascinating.

Above all, Mosel and Saar Rieslings represent the category 'fruity diversity,' since the conditions for growth are ideal here. However, also along the Nahe, in some sites of the Mittelrhein and in the Rheingau such wines can emerge in ideal years and in appropriate soils. The river valleys protect against cool winds, and the slopes, which are mainly facing south, are superbly suited for optimum reception of sunlight. The sparser, more stony slate soil offers an ideal substrate, it stores the warmth of the sun and causes the Riesling vines to bury their roots deep, so as to gather the important minerals from the soil. The grapes can remain hanging on the vines until well into November, thus forming sufficient fruit aromas.

The long vegetation period with an appropriate ripening period is a requirement to ensure that such a delicate yet nevertheless flavor-explosive Riesling with low alcohol content, of 7 to 10% vol., can emerge. Such a diverse development of fruit with a finely subtle sweetness, delicate acidity and such low alcohol content is unique in the world.

Eva Clüsserath
Weingut Ansgar Clüsserath

That Eva Clüsserath ultimately became a winemaker has to do with water, more precisely, with mineral water. Her original intention was to study drinks technology, but after a period of practical training with a drinks corporation, she finally gave up this idea. If drinks, then wine.

She is linked to Riesling in a number of ways. After studies in winemaking, she took over the management of the VDP, the Union of German Prädikat and Qualitätswein estates, in the Pfalz, and is, as she says herself, a "maid of all work." In addition there is her parent's business in Trittenheim in which, since 2001, she has taken on more and more responsibility in the cellar. And then there are the real affairs of the heart, which take her to Westhofen in Rheinhessen, to a wine-estate naturally.

"I commute between Mosel, Pfalz and Rheinhessen, and everywhere I encounter Riesling in ever new variations. I prefer the conventional method of developing my Mosel Rieslings, in order to leave enough room for the characteristics of the slaty soil alongside the clear fruit. My father could no longer understand me, but all I wanted to do was make Mosel Riesling as it used to be made: In the traditional manner!"

And it worked. The Rieslings of the young, graduate winemaker are lacy and yet expressive, the fruit presents itself packed in an exquisite freshness, peppered with that typical slate minerality, as it is to be found along the Mosel. "Riesling is simply a lot of fun, because it can be so refreshingly and uncomplicatedly complicated," says Eva Clüsserath and quite casually accepts that her significant-other, Philipp Wittmann from Westhofen, rather prefers dry wines. The main thing is, Riesling.

Nik Weis

WEINGUT SANKT URBANS-HOF

Nik Weis is one of the most congenial characters to be found in the young winemaking generation in the Mosel region, and furthermore, one of the most successful. He took over his parents' wine estate in Leiwen about ten years ago and brought a new boost of energy into the 40-hectare business. Naturally with Rieslings, which his father and grandfather had planted in the best sites along the Saar and Mosel.

"In good years, the best Mosel wines come from the Saar. Slender, elegant and racy, and not forgetting the fruit, which gives the wine its body. Riesling winemakers are collectors of aromas: the more multilayered and nuance-rich the fruit is in its presentation, the more finesse-rich the interplay with the acid. This is the strength of the variety, and my ambition as a winemaker is to make this strength tastable in the wine. Naturally there are also dry growths on the Sankt Urbans-Hof estate, but the quite clear-cut aim is to produce fresh-fruity, stimulating Rieslings with residual sweetness and relatively little alcohol. Dry Mosel Riesling can be good, but Mosel Riesling with residual sweetness is always good. For Mosel wine, a fruity sweetness simply belongs to it. It is an element of style like the fizzy effervescence in Champagne. With its slender, fruity Rieslings, the Mosel is without competition in the world and thus also competitive."

When the natural conditions of a vintage permit, Nik Weis is pleased about botrytized

Already in his early years, Nik Weis was a constant factor in the Mosel region

Trockenbeerenauslese wines. Although he prefers the easy-drinking, heady Rieslings with a fresh fruit that are consumed with pleasure and delight and which bring into the glass a piece of the landscape in which they are grown. In his case, this can certainly be a vineyard on the Saar.

Dr. Manfred Prüm

WEINGUT JOH. JOS. PRÜM

When Dr. Manfred Prüm receives guests in his fortress-like late-19th-century villa situated

Eva Clüsserath stands for Riesling with a clear Mosel profile

113

directly on the bank of the Mosel, then, naturally Riesling is proffered. However, not just any Riesling from the current vintage. "Young wines are fun, mature wines are multilayered and disclose more of themselves," says Dr Prüm, while he carefully pours.

To guess the vintage, as Dr. Prüm anticipates with a relaxed countenance, is difficult even for practiced wine drinkers, very difficult. Prüm's Rieslings are long-distance runners that are never out of breath, which, even after decades, show not the slightest signs of tiredness or jading. "Rieslings are more lively at the mature stage. My wines are conceived to mature," says Manfred Prüm, and it sounds like a mental link in order to guess the vintage after all. Ten, fifteen or twenty years, who wants to commit themselves? In any case, this winemaker is known for his generous use of his treasure chest.

"Mosel is elegance! The diversity of the fruity aromas, the alternating nuances, and in addition the matching interplay of acidity and a touch of elegant residual sweetness – quite simply irresistible!"

Prüm's Rieslings are ultra-fine works of art, and they are dedicated to fruitiness, and even after several years they never run the risk of tending to a fruitless character or being without body, let alone one-dimensionally gambling away their beguiling charm.

"The composition of the wine should be left to nature, since it can do it better than any modern cellar technology anyway. Anything which has been improved, I don't drink."

Precise opinions, which, out of tradition "Manfred the Great" consistently implements in his wine philosophy. A tour of the cellars is taboo for his guests, although Prüm assures us that there are no secrets in his vinification processes – he just maintains an arm's-length approach.

This little taboo is only one small piece of the mosaic which makes up the myth and the fascination surrounding this tradition-rich estate. Prüm's wine concept is very much alive in the ripened Rieslings, which carry their multilayered fruit aromas like a crown, and with precise accents ennoble the wine to a top-quality growth.

Florian Weingart
WEINGUT WEINGART

Father Weingart still used to let his Riesling ferment spontaneously. His son Florian was of another opinion:

One of the promising winemaker talents in the Mittelrhein region: Florian Weingart

Characterized by slate, the steep Bopparder Hamm vineyard guarantees mineral Rieslings

"I was convinced of the application of cultured yeasts and cool fermentation, because they introduced a glorious freshness and fruitiness into the Rieslings. As a young winemaker it was not quite so clear to me that I could in the process be interfering with the natural structure as a whole. Today, I believe wild yeasts add much to the complexity and to the development potential of a wine."

Florian Weingart is self-critical: "Perhaps I have sometimes gone beyond my objective, and overshot. An idea has been following me concerning natural wine, the reference to nature and the relationship for the complete system. This begins with the selection of our groceries and continues with my work in the vineyard."

He has not yet reached his target, but his Rieslings have already become modest works of art, which excitingly relate fruit and acidity. Such as for example his Spätlese wines from the stony slate Feuerlay and Ohlenberg lots in the legendary Bopparder Hamm.

"Riesling is my wine. It possesses an incredibly wide spectrum, which on the one hand is complicated, but on the other hand is interesting. To be able to develop Riesling in all flavoral tendencies is a real challenge."

Year after year, Florian Weingart takes on these challenges. The young vintner produces up to 14 different Spätlese wines with site designations.

"What the soil yields is important. Only after a certain stage of ripeness does the place of origin come to the fore. A very particular flavor appears with healthy, ripe yields. Picking must therefore take place at an appropriately late moment. In terms of potential, the off-dry and sweet wines along the Mittelrhein are easier for us to produce. The crisp acidity structure sometimes makes it difficult to suitably incorporate the alcohol and the fruit in the dry wines. I love the dry Rieslings, because they are a great challenge for every wine-maker. Although I do not like to lose sight of the residual-sweet Spätlese wines."

Florian Weingart is not content if he is confined by one style, and this is what makes his further career so exciting. "Do you need to determine Rieslings by type in any case? A wine type grows and is not made," he says, full of conviction.

Wilhelm, Thomas and Oliver Haag

WEINGUT
FRITZ HAAG – DUSEMONDER HOF
WEINGUT SCHLOSS LIESER

Only after tasting the Rieslings from the estates of Fritz Haag and Schloss Lieser, is it possible to determine whether talents can be inherited. The wines of Wilhelm Haag have for decades been in the national and international major league, and thus both sons, Thomas and Oliver, have followed directly in the footsteps of the Moselian "old master", without losing touch with the soil under their feet. Wilhelm Haag is proud of his two talented juniors and knows that his wine philosophy is in good hands. Is this the beginning of a successful Mosel wine dynasty?

Only a few miles away from their native Brauneberg, Thomas Haag, together with his wife Ute, have reactivated the Schloss Lieser estate and in no time led it into the top-quality sector of the Mosel region. Light, finesse-rich Riesling, without having to forgo flavor, this is close to the heart of this young wine-making couple. And it is just what they make: gloriously fresh Rieslings which, alongside minerality, possess an exhilarating, delicate fruit diversity and at the same time also express a deep elegance, without making a show of alcohol levels. "The Kabinett style is very important, and I would not like to abandon

Year after year, the Brauneberg Juffer Sonnenuhr top-quality site produces discreetly fruity, delicate Rieslings

it," says Thomas Haag. "spick and span vinification in stainless steel and carried out without too much technology."

This crystal-clear fruitiness also distinguishes his Spätlese wines. Above all the Rieslings from the slaty Brauneberger Juffer Sonnenuhr site present themselves even more clearly via their fruit than do the wines from the somewhat earth-richer Lieser sites. "Only the Riesling can work out these fine fruity distinctions," says Thomas Haag.

Oliver, his brother – who has just joined their parents' estate in Brauneberg – is also of this opinion. Even so, the éminence grise will not be thinking of retirement for a long time. Wilhelm Haag is too much of a personality to withdraw to the quieter life.

"I have left all of the fashions of flavor to one side, since the soil delivers the guidelines for my wine style, and I have to fit myself into these. Brauneberg is not suited to great dry wines. It won't work."

Nor need it. Haag's residual-sweet Rieslings are of such a shining quality and brilliance that one could almost forget that there are such things as dry wines. "Concentration of fruit and finesse, without being too big and prominent, in contrast, pure lightness with a shot of minerality. No one can imitate these residual sweet Rieslings," and father and son agree on this point. For Oliver Haag the classic Mosel wines are therefore "interesting enough, in order to keep the estate on the tried and tested course. We shall remain light and lacy."

This would then really be the beginning of a successful wine dynasty, and the signs are good. Indeed, there was until now always reliance on the Haag wines' exceptional consistency of quality.

Andreas Spreitzer brought new acclaim to the Rheingau family business

Andreas Spreitzer

WEINGUT JOSEF SPREITZER

Naturally, one knows of the Spreitzer estate, since everyone who drives along the road between Oestrich and Winkel automatically looks at the two striking houses. Since the end of the 1990s at the latest, the wines of this Rheingau family business have also been well-known. At that time Andreas Spreitzer brought his Rieslings to the attention of many, and slowly but surely pulled himself up into the top group of the Rheingau winemakers. A talented and successful young winemaker, who together with his brother has revamped the estate of his father. There were always good wines to be had from the Spreitzers, but now the brothers have advanced considerably. *"Rheingau wines do not always need to be dry, a little residual sweetness also suits the Riesling from our locality. It ultimately depends on the soil as to how the grapes taste. One needs to monitor the vineyard very precisely and preferably keep a meticulous account of its particularities and the growth in each plot. Only when I understand what happens there, do I decide in which direction to vinify the wines. A certain proportion of iron and of gravel, which provide for a high measure of minerality, allows an especially fine, residual-sweet Riesling to grow in the Eiserberg."* Andreas Spreitzer calls it "303", following a legendary must weight which his grandfather achieved in this vineyard. That was in 1920, and there were about 600 liters of this botrytized wine. Since 2000, this facet-rich, residual-sweet Spätlese from the old vineyard site of Eiserberg, which in 1867 had already been charted on the Prussian estate map, has been called "303". Andreas Spreitzer is not allowed to use the name Eiserberg, because land consolidation measures have meant that all the plots are subsumed under Oestrich Lenchen.

"303" is an ingenious interplay of sweetness, acidity and fruit, spontaneously fermented, refreshing to the palate, and it carries a hint of the finesse-rich Mosel style. "But the main thing is Riesling, since it displays its first-class abilities in many variations, in all areas and re-gions of the world, and still everyone knows what to expect. Precisely, Riesling."

Daniel and Martha Gantenbein
WEINGUT GANTENBEIN

Martha and Daniel Gantenbein are as well known in the international wine scene as the proverbial village pump. This is due not only to the unmistakable Swiss accent, which is seldom heard in such circles. The extraordinary Pinots Noirs of this winemaking couple are sought after and enjoy enormous popularity. In addition, the Gantenbeins are known as real persons-of-pleasure and absolute quality

The Swiss Daniel Gantenbein is an institution and a committed Riesling fan

fanatics, and on the side as committed Riesling freaks as well. It is not only that they like to drink Riesling as part of their lifestyle, but they also cultivate the variety themselves. This makes them exotics, indeed, the little village of Fläsch, the northernmost community in Grisons canton, is not really considered as one of the Riesling strongholds, and certainly not at all for Rieslings in the residual-sweet Mosel style. "Naturally, at some point in our wine drinking we discovered Riesling, to be precise, Mosel Rieslings," says Martha Gantenbein. She still exactly recalls the key experience. "It was a 1983 Maximin Grünhäuser Abtsberg Riesling-Auslese," a taste experience with consequences. "We asked ourselves whether such a wine would also be possible here at home," says Daniel Gantenbein. "Not a copy, but a light, elegant Riesling with residual sweetness in the style of the Mosel. We bought Riesling vines on the Mosel and planted them in the Wiesli site, a small vineyard at an altitude of 1800 feet with a very Spartan slaty soil and without any humus. Naturally, at the beginning, we anxiously asked: Whatever will emerge from this soil? The answer came in 1997 with the first Riesling. Mineral-rich, fruity wines with fine slaty notes. We define the residual sweetness purely in terms of taste, that is, without recourse to analysis results." The Gantenbeins' residual-sweet Rieslings are only available in Spätlese or Auslese quality.

"We would like to establish ourselves somewhat with Riesling and as Swiss winemakers, and naturally it is a homage to a very special grape variety. It is our dream to be able to make a Beerenauslese just once, but in our climate we hardly ever experience botrytis. Although actually Riesling is good in all quality grades, it can be relatively simple and nevertheless display finesse and playfulness. It must simply taste good to us, and then we shall consider it a good wine."

Hermann J. Wiemer

HERMANN J. WIEMER VINEYARD

In truth, Hermann Wiemer cannot deny his roots. The native Moselian emigrated to the USA in 1968 and a few years later he founded a winery and established vine cultivation on the western side of Seneca Lake. No wonder that Rieslings play a role in his business, after all, Hermann Wiemer grew up in Bernkastel. He cultivates today about 18 hectares of vineyards, from which came the first dry Rieslings of the Finger Lakes region. "Wines in the European tradition," he quite self-confidently calls his products, for which Riesling fans in the New World sometimes queue up.

Despite the popularity of his wines and the awards such as "Winery of the Year 2003", Hermann Wiemer has remained down-to-earth. He carries out a majority of the work himself, and he actively takes part in the harvesting as well. Not a winery manager in a business suit, rather the winemaker from the Mosel with a direct connection to the product. Under the name of Johannisberg-Riesling he produces dry and off-dry qualities, as well as juicy Spätlese wines and, if nature allows, also ice wines. It would certainly be somewhat of an exaggeration to speak of an imported Mosel style. However, from the fruitiness of the Rieslings, partly from botrytized grapes, it is possible to recognize that he has found a new home here, without disguising the fact that he comes from the classic Riesling country.

COMPLEX ELEGANCE

The great dry Rieslings

The terms "complex" and "elegant" appear time and again in descriptions of wine. When both attributes relate to a Riesling, there arises as a rule a great, extract-rich wine with profundity and character, which is certainly among those most in demand but also among the most difficult to make.

Reduced yields and a strict selection during the harvest are a precondition. Indeed, the concentration of flavor in the ripe grapes and thereby in the fruit body counts for more than the mandatory must weight. Healthy grapes without rot guarantee the shining elegance and are a prerequisite for Rieslings of this type: they are a synthesis of fruit, vigor, complexity and elegance.

These wines often present themselves in their youth as still uncommunicative and simply hint at a hidden idea of their complexity. The nose initially receives a discreet impression from rich, often still reluctant, fragrant impressions and from the facet-rich aroma dimensions which conceal themselves in the bouquet. Such Rieslings impart an entire fount of different aromas, which rest finely-layered upon one another and complement one another, without coming across as ponderous on the olfactory nerves, let alone florid. The sense of taste inevitably wants to capture and assign this diversity, to get behind every individual aroma and name it. The attempt is inevitably made to classify the multi-layered,

complex bouquet in one's own filing system of smells and aromas, in order to understand the wine accordingly.

The complexity lies in the perfect integration of the various elements and in the linking of various parts to a whole, indeed to a fruit and aroma cocktail, which is constructed in an extremely multifaceted way. Some backbone is sought here, a solid acidity structure which underscores the lacy quality, the brilliance and the profundity of the Riesling and holds them together in a solid, complex structure.

ELEGANCE AND COUNTENANCE

The elegance that imparts self-confident reserve to this complexity is the second important component of this category. How do nose and palate receive the aromas, with what intensity does the Riesling present itself? With a certain countenance, without forfeiting aromatic attentiveness at the same time! The clear fruit aromas are supported by the flavor-carrier of alcohol, which weighs neither massively nor burdensomely on the structure of the wine, but in moderate percentages, introduces to the Riesling a flavoral dynamism and a distinctive taste which is inevitably associated with the word elegance.

PATIENCE IS EVERYTHING

Complex and elegant Rieslings demand the passion and the patience of the winemaker. The long growth period which Riesling finds in the northern cultivation zones offers the chance to exploit the physiological ripeness of the grapes to the full without the sugar levels shooting up at the same time, which would, with fermentation, result in a high alcohol content. The later the moment of harvest, the nearer the grapes come to full ripeness, and all the more distinct and intensive is the development of the aromas, which impart to this wine style the desired elegance and the extraordinary, flavoral, multifaceted character.

It is a slow but steady ripening, which always entails the danger of a sudden rot infestation – especially as the end of the mild autumnal weather gets ever closer. Therefore these great Rieslings are very often obtained at the limits of feasibility.

For the winemaker, it's all or nothing, since in these all-decisive weeks, everything can be lost. It is an uninterrupted high-wire act, and it is not for nothing that winemakers have dedicated themselves to precisely this Riesling style, because they love this constant challenge. And they succeed in producing elegant, complex wine-personalities year after year, despite changing climatic conditions and other imponderables.

These elegant, vigorous – and as a rule, dry – wines possess longevity and furthermore they go especially well with food. Indeed, the well-accentuated alcohol, the delicate acidity structure and the complexity and multilayered aromas offer a flavoral, self-assured counterbalance to many dishes.

Philipp Wittmann

WEINGUT WITTMANN

Philipp Wittmann makes a congenial impression. A good-looking young man with stature and style. Someone from whose appearance the arduous work of the vineyards is not to be deduced, one would not suspect the winemaker in him. Firstly, his wines must be tasted, in order to get to know the winegrower and to understand his ideas about everything under the sun, and his feelings about the vineyard and his homeland, Rheinhessen. Philipp Wittmann laughs if you almost reproachfully mention the region's name to him. "The homeland is the challenge to make something

new out of the traditional," he says, and it sounds quite convincing all around. The young winemaker has built up one of the best Riesling addresses in Rheinhessen, indeed in all Germany, from the long-established family business on the edge of town in Westhofen. The basis for his success – he presented his first wine in 1999 – was however created by his father and grandfather. Their wines are now stored in nice neat rows in the treasure chamber in the old cellar vaults. "As a winemaker I can really experiment wildly," he says, "it offers me an unimaginable flexibility and the possibility to implement my ideas in a confined space." Half of his vine area is planted with Riesling, which he cares for according to strict biodynamic principles.

"Dry wines can better document our terroir, because Riesling in this style finds the right words and talks of its place of origin. I see my task as a winemaker in the patience to let the Rieslings simply happen, so that they can tell something of their place of origin, and thereby also of me."

It is these elegant, complex Rieslings from the Westhofen Morstein site which Philipp Wittmann uses as a mouthpiece for his talent. Wines which appear compact, which take a hold, which connect. Wines which distribute their structure equally, over a fine minerality, a ripened fruit and a pleasing acidity. "In 25 years I will know if I was on the right track with my Rieslings," he says, although he knows very well that his Riesling can be downright addictive. A humble understatement, typical for Rheinhessen. There are many things going on here with regard to Riesling.

Pacesetter of quality in Rheinhessen: Philipp Wittmann

Hansjörg Rebholz has set a new course in the southern Pfalz

Hansjörg Rebholz
Weingut Ökonomierat Rebholz

"The southern Pfalz is situated nearer to Alsace than to the Rheingau. Perhaps we simply represent a flavoral style between the two: vigorous, dense, and at the same time complex and elegant. Rieslings do not allow themselves to be simply squeezed into a regional formula, they are much more a reflection of different factors. With Riesling I can work out the entire components of a vineyard – that is to say, soil, climate, topogra-

phy and geographical site – so that one can smell and taste the place of origin. Above all, I am convinced that the site – that is, the place where the vines have their roots, in the truest sense of the word – characterizes the wine. Of course there is in addition all that happens to the soil: how does water pass through the soil, what are the wind characteristics, and how are the influences of the weather perceived? In addition, it depends on the craft skill of the winegrowers as to how they deal with these parameters and how they interpret what nature dictates. Although these effects vary from year to year, the characteristic of the site should be without doubt tastable. It is a question of recognizability. I find it fascinating, when the Kastanienbusch can be tasted and named as a vineyard site. Only in the last few years has it actually become clear to me how important the differences are with Riesling. I try more and more to give Riesling a mineral note, because I can thereby most efficiently define its place of origin. With my wines I have always placed emphasis on longevity. There is much evidence as to how fantastically wines age when they have been produced in this way. Today, I don't really do anything different from the methods of my father and grandfather. In some points however, I try to perfect my work. The basic requirement is uncompromisingly clean harvested produce. And this involves a lot of time and work in the vineyard. Only then can wines evolve which are long-lasting and can further develop while aging. The aroma of my Rieslings must be comprehensible, it must constitute the character of the wine and produce the excitement which leads to a desire for a second and a third sip, even after many years."

Werner Schönleber
WEINGUT EMRICH-SCHÖNLEBER

He is an old hand in the Riesling world and has achieved almost all that can be achieved in the life of a winemaker. Werner Schönleber is one of the contemplative German top-class winemakers who continually scrutinize their work, although particularly their Rieslings are of such overpowering clarity and elegance that suddenly you would prefer just to forget about all else. He calls it "drinking pleasure" and "Even Goethe found pleasure in Monzinger Rieslings. My wines are never broad and prominent, they flow lean over the tongue, stimulate in the middle part and bow out with a mineral aftertaste. All these together should encourage drinking, since that's why wine is made."

Werner Schönleber: guarantor of complex, elegant Rieslings with outstanding potential

Werner Schönleber produced his first vintage in 1971, when he was only 19 years old. Since then he has permanently advanced, and today is among the best in his trade. Year by year, he offers the wine world top-class collections, from the simple Gutsriesling (estate Riesling) to the elegant Grosse Gewächse (grands crus) right up to finesse-rich botrytized wines.

"Monzingen was always known for Riesling, sometimes more, sometimes less. I grew up here with Riesling and have seen that on the steep, dry slopes nothing other than Riesling can grow. The hunger-artist Riesling is frugal, though it exhibits in the glass its nuance-rich diversity: pure minerality, a piquant, smooth, almost polished acidity, including delicately fruity, immensely multilayered aromas with complex elegance."

Whoever can wait some years will find out that particularly with Schönleber's mature, ample, dry Rieslings, the pleasure of drinking is especially great.

Heinrich Breuer manages one of the best-known German estates

Heinrich Breuer
Weingut Georg Breuer

Burgundy, Montpellier, Canada, the USA: the brothers Heinrich and Bernhard Breuer were already on the move in the wine business in the early 1960s. "Back then we didn't understand everything, much was new to us, and some things we had simply never seen before on our parents' estate. However, our time spent abroad characterized our wine methods." In addition to these, there is certainly the idea of the "cru-vineyards," to which the Rüdesheim top-quality sites of Rottland, Roseneck and Schlossberg belong. Not forgetting the Nonnenberg in Rauenthal, a vineyard whose history stretches back to the 12th century.

"All Riesling crus are aged traditionally in wood. The possibility of an exchange of oxygen, which is excluded by steel tanks, makes the Rieslings more complex in their fruit, more stable in their structure and allows them to mature better. If however, we have the feeling that the influence of wood is becoming too great for the Riesling, the wine is then briefly stored elsewhere in steel. Riesling reacts immediately to the slightest changes. The winemaker must create ideal conditions for Riesling, so that it can mature. It will then exhibit a great flavoral diversity and the differences between the individual sites can be distinctly discerned. Sometimes it is only a matter of 100 yards. It can even be tasted in the grapes shortly before picking. If it is not interfered with, the Riesling will always retain the character of its vineyard. Looked at that way, it has a true soul that

never denies where it comes from. My favorite is the Rüdesheimer Berg Schlossberg, maybe also because it is the most difficult site that we possess. In contrast the Nonnenberg reacts rather more unproblematically. A lot of work and effort, but also thought must be invested in the Schlossberg site, in order to be rewarded at harvest time. Real masterpieces of the hillside which Riesling uses to express its terroir in the wine. Since 1980, the Schlossberg Rieslings have been supplied with labels designed by artists. This was my brother's idea and we will continue this tradition in future. The Rüdesheimer Berg Schlossberg 2002 was also the last wine he vinified before his sudden death." One of the many viticultural pièces de résistance that commemorate the great Riesling winemaker Bernhard Breuer.

Andreas Laible
WEINGUT ANDREAS LAIBLE

Baden is not particularly considered as one of the Riesling strongholds among the German vine growing regions, although the wine village of Durbach is traditionally closely linked to Riesling. In former times, the vine was known here as Klingelberger, and the wines were classically developed with a light sweetness. "That simply made the Rieslings more palatable," explains Andreas Christian. He graduated in wine technology and then completed a training period with Willi Bründlmayer in Kamptal before joining his parents' business. "My father also altered his Riesling style in view of the increasing preference for dry wines in the 1990s. We discovered that a drier Riesling, freed from an overlying sweetness, can much better express its gloriously intense minerality."

After these experiences, Andreas Laible devoted himself entirely to dry Riesling and in the last few years he has become a Riesling star in Baden. "I am looking for brilliant, flawless Rieslings that are completely unadulterated," and he is working on this meticulously. Little by little, the wooden vats were removed from the cellar and replaced with steel tanks. "We have available many different container sizes, so as to be able to individually develop each parcel of land. With seven hectares, that involves an enormous amount of work on the steep, rocky Plauelrain site.

"Important to us is the diversity that Riesling can offer. This is why we have planted appropriate clones from other areas which, for us, conjure up the desired delicacy into Riesling. The hot summer of 2003 for instance was a perfect Mosel year in Plauelrain: the vines produced more acidity of their own accord, which had a glorious, lively influence. We no longer want to operate according to the book, we are, rather, more in search of something new, something which not everyone is doing."

Toni Bodenstein
WEINGUT PRAGER

It is difficult to find a suitable description to fit Toni Bodenstein. He is a walking encyclopedia on the subjects of geology, terroir, history and culture, and a constant warning voice pointing out the genetic impoverishment that results from new clones. "The old vines understand the soil in all its variety," says Toni Bodenstein. His elegant Rieslings from the vineyards of Steinriegl, Kaiserberg, Achleiten and Klaus, are very sophisticated, fruit-complex masterpieces with a fine miner-

The Wachau region is not only a world cultural heritage site, but also a world-famous wine region with its own identity

ality. They are tasty representatives from the depths of the volcanic soil. Real Bodenstein wines.

"I would like to put the countenance of Riesling into the bottle and to develop elegance and finesse, particularly where there are poor substrates with little topsoil. Our seven different Smaragd-quality wines are therefore images of their respective sites. They are designed to show how differently Riesling is characterized by the soil formations and the subtle micro-climate without the need for any touching up."

In the tradition-rich Prager estate, these are not always dry wines. About ten years ago, Toni Bodenstein produced the first Trockenbeerenauslese in the Wachau region.

"It is important that we give Riesling a chance to demonstrate the maximum from its repertoire.

If the intention is to create a Riesling region of worldwide importance, one must also be able to develop extremes and to exhibit top-class sweet botrytized wines. The thrill of this variety is precisely how differently it grows in the various regions of Europe and in contrast to the New World. The old regions have an independence which they must keep. On our steep sites, individuality triumphs: here the vine and the winemaker are required to wrest, from difficult conditions, a wine that conveys what the Wachau region constitutes. Riesling likes to have a little torment, it doesn't like luxury. The intelligent winemaker demonstrates a readiness to take a risk and leaves to nature what others add in the cellar."

The Wachau region is a World Cultural Heritage site and thus more than just a place for tourist excursions. It is, as Herr Bodenstein says, "A world wine region, which is not only permitted to live out its identity, but is required to pass it on."

Martin Nigl
WEINGUT MARTIN NIGL

Some years ago at a blind tasting, there was a surprise winner, still relatively unknown in Germany. The Nigl estate in the small Priel community in the Austrian Kremstal region left the competition looking pale and clearly convinced the highly distinguished jury of its significance. That was not the first time that Martin Nigl had quietly driven his highly estimated colleagues from the field. For years, with impressive continuity, this estate has been producing Rieslings and of outstanding quality, which only develop their great form over time.

"Fruit-accentuated, smooth, mineral Rieslings that are not too opulent. This represents my wine vision. The wines must live from their delicate fruit and elegant complexity."

Martin Nigl has ideal conditions to realize his vision and put it into practice. A few miles north of Krems, his terraced vineyard sites snuggle up against the gentle slopes.

"The primitive rock soils ensure sufficient minerality. Along with the presence of minerality, the strength of the Riesling is its prominent fruit, which – in the best case – it presents as clear as a bell and as sharp as a knife. Since we wish to exhibit this, our Rieslings undergo reductive aging in steel tanks."

The Nigls are a real family business. His son Josef is responsible for the management and the upkeep of the vineyards, his wife Christine – together with her husband – caters for the necessary marketing of the wines. The parents, Josef and Gisela, laid the foundation stone for their success and still help out if need be.

"We are inclined to wish for our Rieslings to be on the dry side, although they are more delicate and leaner than the opulent Wachau equivalents. Despite a high aging potential these Rieslings close up at some point and lie dormant for some years. However, one thing is certain: they wake up again and reward those with patience!"

Jeffrey Grosset
GROSSET WINES

At the beginning of the 1980s when Jeffrey Grosset founded his estate, he had one thing clearly in his sights: absolute top quality. Initially not an absurd demand for an Australian winemaker, but he wanted to produce a wine whose character should be clearly distinguished by the interplay of variety and terroir. Why not then a Riesling?

Today, Jeffrey Grosset produces the finest dry Rieslings on the fifth continent, of course in a suitable climate and in suitable soils. "Even though the wine world hardly took notice of Australian Riesling at that time, today it belongs without any doubt in the worldwide Riesling scene, and the potential is nowhere near to being exhausted." We can therefore expect to be hearing much more about Australian Rieslings.

What Jeffrey Grosset has hitherto accomplished is really impressive. His Polish Hill Riesling is a thoroughly vigorous wine, whose straightforward structure elegantly integrates the fine-fruity classic aromas of Australian Rieslings. It grows in stony slate soils interspersed with quartzite, lime and loam. "There is maturing potential within it, even years later Riesling plays out its strengths and shines with ripened fruit, honey and the typical lime flavor." Only hand-picked, ripe grapes from a late harvest are used for the wine. In some years botrytis develops in the vineyards, and the Rieslings display a fine residual sweetness. In order to ensure fruitiness and elegance, Jeffrey Grosset ages his Rieslings exclusively in steel tanks. All the wines are marketed with screw caps. He believes that particularly the fine-fruity varieties such as Riesling and Sauvignon Blanc which are low in extract are highly susceptible to cork problems. This is an example of simple, perhaps even unorthodox modernity in developments in the wine industry, which the traditional wine consumer in old Europe must first learn to deal with in a laid-back fashion.

Pierre Trimbach produces the legendary Clos Ste Hune

Pierre Trimbach
Weingut F. E. Trimbach

Clos Ste Hune is an Alsatian and one of the most famous Rieslings in the world. Actually, it should be called Grand Cru Rosacker, named after its place of origin north of Hunawihr, a small village between Ribeauvillé and Riquewihr. Since 1919 the Rieslings from this parcel of land, only just over a hectare in size, have been marketed under the name of Clos Ste Hune, although the vineyard is not an official "Clos" in the Burgundian sense. However, it is delimited by a low wall, and it is under this name that the wine has become a well-known worldwide brand. A sensitive, elegant Riesling which tells you its place of origin unasked and possesses an almost endless maturing ability – even in apparently bad years. The vines are planted in muschelkalk and lettenkeuper, which imparts a slightly spicy pepper bouquet to the wine. Pierre Trimbach thinks it important to point out the aging time of the wine:

"With increasing age, the aroma is rounded off and expresses elegant, multilayered and above all mineral notes. Unfortunately there is too little Clos Ste Hune to satisfy the worldwide demand. The yield fluctuates with each vintage. What is constant however is the exceptional potential which the Riesling extracts from its terroir. Clos Ste Hune is a great, dry, very elegant wine. It displays its real grandeur only after a few years. We sell it about four years after the harvest. Anyone who can then wait another few years will be presented with a unique, complex and elegant fruit, and in addition a finely adjusted acidity that the Riesling is able to extract from this little piece of earth."

BAROQUE MONUMENTS

Playful impetus and strength

When Rieslings are depicted as "Baroque monuments", then something awesome resonates in this description. As a rule, monuments are enormous and prominent memorials with symbolic character. Monuments impress themselves upon a place and appear to be made for eternity. If Baroque stylistic elements are included, then the attention of the observer is addressed with lavish, complicated ornaments in sweeping curves. This almost ebullient obsession with detail usually dissolves however, into an impressively clear overall view.

There are Rieslings which – like musical instruments – possess a sounding board that leaves sufficient space for all these vibrations to resonate. Luscious Rieslings, which similarly display grandeur, impetus and playfulness, and leave their mark on the memory, because they deploy their fascinating brilliance only slowly and carefully. It is the depth of the wine which characterizes the monumental quality, a depth which can initially appear immobile, excessive, almost ponderous, but gains freshness with increasing maturity in the bottle. Baroque Riesling monuments do not promise uncomplicated and easy drinking pleasure. These Rieslings possess opulent vibrancy, their vigor is consolidated in well-proportioned exuberance which they noticeably bring to the fore, although not with playful aromas and crisp acidity, but with immensely fruity characteristics and pompous affectation. Full-bodied and substantial on the palate, whoever wishes to experience their real grandeur must acquiesce in the usurping influence of this wine, accept the alcohol and enjoy the juicy opulence that rolls around the tongue.

That these Rieslings do not originate in light soils goes almost without saying. The vigorous character of the wine requires geological soil structures that contain sufficient substance and above all minerals. Primitive rock, gneiss, granite, loess and loam are therefore perfectly able to impart the necessary strength of character in these baroque Rieslings. In addition there is the individual personal imprint and the talent of the winemaker to suitably express the Riesling and thus also the terroir.

It is often the case that winemakers reflect their lifestyle in their wines, and introduce into Riesling a part of themselves. This can be displayed in various styles – old fashioned classic, such as the "Saumagen" by Bernd Philippi as well as the mineral, fruity, firm Riesling, such as "Idig" by Steffen Christmann or even the noticeably botrytis-affected, and thus somewhat short on minerality, such as the "Vinothekenfüllung" by Emmerich Knoll or the "Unendlich" by F. X. Pichler from the Wachau region.

In any case, the Rieslings of this category are long-lived because they usually possess sufficient, substantial fitness to outlast generations of insignificant, trendy wines. This doesn't mean that they must demonstrate their real grandeur in their first year and certainly not with the first sip. Patience is required, passion for wines which will remain long in one's memory. One must devote oneself to monuments in order to understand the idea and the personal imprint of the winemaker. They must be given time to develop. In their youth they often taste very appealing but then descend into a period of Sleeping-Beauty slumber, only to reawaken more radiant than ever.

Steffen Christmann

Weingut A. Christmann

"It is not possible to make special wines if one simply just goes on producing. Wine must proceed in conformity with life, both must be harmonious in themselves. Individual flavors should at the same time be brought into harmony with tradition," says Steffen Christmann and he means Riesling above all other varieties. "It is simply wonderful to see the facets in which Riesling can generate dance-like elegant wines, and it can do this despite the vigor and opulence which the Pfalz Riesling contains by nature. Riesling is never tiring if one correctly understands and accepts it."

Steffen Christmann believes the language of the Riesling comes from the terroir. "If the vine is encouraged, then a vineyard can very individually communicate its own characteristic." In order to achieve this aim, Steffen Christmann works according to basic, biodynamic principles.

Recently also an advocate in the field of biodynamics: Steffen Christmann

"One needs to listen in to the vineyard, and positively, naturally activate it, since only then will the various, authentic influences become noticeable. When chemical influences are discontinued, the plant itself will alter. Initially, it will literally droop, but after the change, the vine will recover, it will become stronger, and will extract minerals which it needs from the soil. Naturally, there must be much closer monitoring of the vineyards, which no doubt means higher personnel expenditure. Willingness to compromise is ultimately a form of convenience, and exactly this makes the difference for me: The difference between good and very good."

Steffen Christmann's vineyards are situated all around Gimmeldingen, and one of his best sites is the Königsbacher Idig. "Here, Riesling allows a glimpse into the multilayered structure of its thick, powerful fruit aromas. The wine flexes its muscles, appears almost a little baroque, but the vigor is perfectly integrated and is assisted by a tempting minerality." A prime example of how things interact in order to fit together. That, in addition, the Rieslings have sufficient potential for years to come is what makes them great. It is exactly such wines behind which visionary winemakers are always to be found. For example Steffen Christmann.

Gunter Künstler
Weingut Franz Künstler

"There is so much Chardonnay worldwide, but so little Riesling." Gunter Künstler says this in a regretful tone, and he works hard so that at least the world speaks of first-class Rieslings. Since his first vintage in 1988 the world also speaks of Rieslings from Gunter Künstler. "For me, it is above all a matter of aging capability. Great wines must prove themselves over a long period of time, and this does not only apply to botrytized wines. Dry Rieslings should also provide pleasure and offer enjoyment in the long term." Gunter Künstler not only has the talent, but also the suitable soils to produce real Riesling monuments. In the extreme east of the Rheingau, all around Hochheim, the soils have depth. Alongside sandy, gravelly formations, it is above all the heavy, tertiary, marl soils which

generate substantial, massive wines with breeding and elegance.

"The Rieslings from the Hochheimer Hölle always carry something monumental within them. They require a certain warm-up period to mature, but then, however, they present themselves as multilayered, expressive and above all lasting. Also the Rieslings from the Domdechaney site expect this patience, since they are initially complicated and lacking in charm. However, after a few years they will achieve an impressive grandeur, the potential is there in these wines. As a winemaker, I need only to prepare the stage, so that the wine can perform well and show its strengths. Gut feeling is required as well, and naturally also the necessary craft skills. We winemakers are the bespoke tailors for Riesling, so that in the end, everything fits together. When we achieve this, then the Hochheimer Riesling is un-

Gunter Künstler has been among the world's best Riesling growers for years

beatable in its elegant impetus, playfulness and monumental flavoral sustainability, and it is inimitable. It is like a rainbow, iridescent in many colors, but nevertheless presenting an impressive, enclosed image and above all, lastingly remains in one's memory. It's rather a shame that there are so seldom rainbows and that there is so little Riesling."

Bernd Philippi
WEINGUT KOEHLER-RUPRECHT

Bernd Philippi is one of the most extraordinary protagonists on the German winemaking scene. On the one hand as a flying winemaker and consultant much in demand and on the move around the world, on the other hand he is the ideal image of a down-to-earth winemaker from the Pfalz. An institution, so to speak, with a visible tendency for pleasure and equipped with a suitably sized portion of composure, although often enough he is under pressure of time. However, he always has time for his friends, and he enjoys these moments immensely.
"I am a winemaker who desires to bring the fascination of wine as authentically as possible into the bottle. Patience and commitment are thus required. Nature is not a department store, where items can be ordered and then delivered, and even exchanged if they are not suitable. Passion and humility are the prerequisites for the winemaker's craft. Those who work at a hectic pace and can never wait, have already lost."
This is no lip service. Bernd Philippi allows sufficient time for his Rieslings. Above all, the dry Spätlese and Auslese wines from his Kallstadter Saumagen top-class site with its lime-interspersed soil, have something of the calm

of this congenial winemaker within them. "As the person, so the wine", says Bernd Philippi, "all haste is the work of the devil."
The hale-and-hearty Rieslings achieve their peak only after five or six years. Then they really do stand like monuments in the glass, grandly balanced, vigorous, lusciously concentrated and masterfully presented with a smooth, proportioned acidity.

Hans-Josef Becker
WEINGUT J. B. BECKER

Since the 2003 vintage, there have no longer been any corks at the estate of Hans-Josef Becker in Walluf. Without exception, his wine bottles are sealed with glass stoppers. In other respects, this winegrower, with his striking Kaiser Wilhelm mustache, is less interested in modern methods. On the contrary, he is a traditionalist in the best sense of the word.
"Wine has been made in the Rheingau for 1000 years and it's not necessary to continually tamper with proven methods. I make primarily dry Rheingau Rieslings in the traditional style and today I work much more conservatively than my father. No beautification or correction, no filtration, since these are at the cost of vigor and aromas. There are only wooden vats in my cellar, the Rieslings lie for a long time on the lees, this makes them more stable and gives them a powerful texture. My slogan is: simply let it lie, and wait and see. I have never done anything else."
Hans-Josef Becker usually only brings his body-rich Rieslings from the heavy soils of the Wallufer Walkenberg on to the market after an appropriate aging period. "There are

Adhering entirely to the traditional style: Hans-Josef Becker

Robert Haller
WEINGUT FÜRST LÖWENSTEIN

The Homburger Kallmuth is an imposing monument to nature, and the vineyard is listed as an historic site. Glaciers have carved their way through here left and right, and in between, left standing like an amphitheater, is the Kallmuth vineyard in a bend of the Main river. Wine has been cultivated here on the steep, concave slope for about 900 years. "A sub-Mediterranean climate predominates here on sunny days with baking temperatures of 50 to 60°C," explains Robert Haller, manager and winemaker on Prince Löwenstein's estate. Homburger Kallmuth has been in the sole ownership of this princely house since 1872. Each year about €300,000 has to be invested to maintain the dry-stone walling of the terraces – an enormous investment for a very special vineyard. "It is a unique site, massive and impressive, it is, however, above all prepossessing. It is captivating like a theater play and one hopes it will go on and on." The soil is interspersed with variegated sandstone and overlying muschelkalk. "Altogether the result is a unique basis for vigorous, decidedly earthy wines of high minerality. Those who have scented these rocks on hot or humid days will also rediscover the scent in the wine."

This is usually the beginning of a friendship with the wines from the monument of Kallmuth.

"You have to be crazy and love this vineyard insanely, it eats up so much energy and working time, but then it gives so much back to us."

Rieslings of stunning grandeur, with an individual character. As impressive as the vineyard from which they come.

wines that we deliberately withhold from sale, and others from which so many bottles are filled that we cannot sell them straight away, and the old vintages in the price list are thus explained. We have already taken over an enormous store from our father, a treasure which signifies economic security," says sister Maria. When one asks about the current vintage, a weary smile is the response. Those who know Hans-Josef Becker know that the current wines still lie in the cellar. However, many Rieslings from the 1990s are available, and even-older treasures on request. "I would never plant anything other than Riesling and Spätburgunder (Pinot Noir) here in the Rheingau. Which variety has so many faces as Riesling? It's a good thing that Riesling has now been rediscovered," says the vintner.

Franz Hirtzberger

WEINGUT FRANZ HIRTZBERGER

"The cool scent of the community of Spitz is present in the Rieslings," says Franz Hirtzberger, and his eyes twinkle even more cunningly than ever. There is no doubt about it: the Rieslings of Singerriedel are vigorous and nevertheless quite delicate, full of minerality and tend to suggest something of the cool climate which sometimes blows across the charming river landscape of the Wachau. "The Wachau region doesn't make it easy for the winemaker, but people develop through their tasks," he believes. "The best site begins directly behind the house, our flagship of

Singerriedel. A highly mineral soil with gneiss and slate, containing iron in some places. Some of the vineyard lots had not been cultivated for decades despite the enormous potential." The Hirtzbergers recognized the opportunities and brought new life to the area. *"Our Rieslings from the Singerriedel vineyard are vinified only in Smaragd quality. This requires a high degree of ripeness, and the botrytized grapes are selectively picked, separately processed and later reintroduced into the mass of the wine which was in the vineyard."*
Franz Hirtzberger handles his wines very carefully: "No improvements, no additives. We intend only to accompany the wine and not to force it in a particular direction," says Franz Hirtzberger who is now assisted by his son, Franz.
The Rieslings of the Hirtzbergers are captivating, with vigorous fruit and fascinating suppleness, which, when so well balanced, is only seldom to be found with Riesling.

F. X. Pichler

WEINGUT F. X. PICHLER

Franz Xaver Pichler has an impressive personality, a winemaker who has cult status, but who prefers not to make a big thing of it or his wines. "In our business we have always had Riesling and Grüner Veltliner, and I have changed nothing in this respect."
Pichler especially values the potential and the ability of the old vines to extract the basics for great wines from the sparse soils of the steep

Two generations of Franz Hirtzberger, but always first-class quality

One of the calm and peaceful Riesling world stars: F. X. Pichler

"Unendlich" (never-ending) and as a label, gave it the legendary 1815 stage-set for the appearance of the Queen of the Night in Mozart's "Magic Flute." A wine that otherwise, in this complex perfection, perhaps only Mozart could have created, if he had been a winegrower. In 1999, Pichler's son Lukas, "inherited" the cellar from his father, and Franz Xaver concentrates on the vineyards. Those grand ideas for wines which the talented junior consistently implements in the cellar, form in his head here in the vineyard.

Willi Bründlmayer
WEINGUT BRÜNDLMAYER

terraces in the Dürnsteiner Kellerberg and Loibner Berg.

"This can only be accomplished if the wine comes into being in advance in one's head. Not so much as a dream, much more as a tangible idea, such as takes maximum advantage of the ripening period of the grapes, in order to introduce vigor and aromatic complexity into the wine. A healthy botrytis, which can give the wine fullness and depth, is not a problem here but a prerequisite." Pichler's 1990 Kellerberg Riesling is legendary, it drove the ever-successful competition from the field at tastings in Paris, London and New York. However, the pinnacle of his career came in 1998 with an extraordinary Riesling. "I had to make this one, because perhaps it would never happen again," says Franz Pichler. He calls his favorite wine

The Kamptal winemaker Willi Bründlmayer is not only an advertisement for this tranquil region, but has been an international emissary for Austrian wines for a long time. It need not always be Grüner Veltliner. Bründlmayer's Rieslings are equally well appreciated worldwide, above all the growths from the Zöbinger Heiligenstein, the geologically oldest and certainly also the most interesting site on the estate. The vineyard has been well known for a long time, but it was the Bründlmayers who first made it famous. Today, the Heiligenstein – along with the Wachauer vineyards – is the most famous Riesling site in Austria, and for Bründlmayer, it is again and again a special challenge:

"The Riesling vines on our terraces are up to 70 years old and hang on a deep and widely ramified root system. For this reason, especially concentrated wines occur here. Furthermore, about a third of our vines are on what is called "lyre-train-

ing", which divides the vine in such a way that it reaches out like two sun-worshipping arms pointing skywards. Like this, the sunlit and aerated leaf surface is almost doubled and the quality of the grapes is improved. In addition, quality also comes from below: the Heiligenstein Rieslings extract their vigor from the sandstone soil which has volcanic elements."

The Riesling selections of fully-ripe and over-ripe grapes are massive, rich in body, very concentrated and have depth, and they always come with an enormous potential of minerality.

Emmerich Knoll
WEINGUT EMMERICH KNOLL

"Wachau Rieslings are classic wines, but cannot be reduced to a common denominator. Great wines are individualists, just like the winemakers who become involved with them." Emmerich Knoll has been doing this for around 30 years and during this time, he has set a course in the wine landscape along the Danube with his Baroque, luscious wines: *"My Rieslings introduce concentration, vigor and the corresponding elegance into the glass. In such an interplay, the terroir, as well as the individual imprint of the business itself must be recognizable. Fundamentally, wines should make a flavoral statement about their place of origin, and also say something about their year of birth."*

Meanwhile, in the Knoll estate, his son, also called Emmerich, is at work, who in turn coordinates all stages in the vineyard and cellar with his father. "The one in charge here is my father, he's the boss," says the young winemaker, who incidentally agrees with his father and prefers the same wine style.

"Prominent in a positive sense, that means to demonstrate a character in a form that does not get out of hand. The Rieslings should by all means bring fullness, but within the limits of suitable elegance. This can be assisted with botrytized grapes if nature allows. Botrytis provides our Rieslings with an additional dimension, namely depth and complexity, and makes them interesting, and above all durable. In particularly good years we even bring out a luscious, botrytis-characterized "vinotheque bottling" which neglects the terroir a little, while in return presenting an unbelievable opulence with a multilayered aroma, guaranteeing a long aging capability. This opulence however, should never be at the expense of elegance, since even great wines must offer drinking pleasure."

Individualists they certainly are, the father, the son and the wine. The striking label of the Knoll wines is as unmistakable as their Rieslings: simply classic!

Laurence Faller
DOMAINE WEINBACH

The Domaine Weinbach is situated shortly before you reach Kaysersberg in Alsace, at the foot of the famous Schlossberg grand cru site, surrounded by a wall, amid vineyards. It is a stately property founded by Capuchin friars and it has been connected with winemaking for centuries. It appears as if the good old times have stood still. In a wood-paneled room with an old tiled stove and a velvet couch, portraits of many generations hang on the walls. They all belong to the Faller family which has been running the domaine for over 100 years. Today, three women are in charge of the estate: Colette Faller and her two daughters Catherine and Laurence. Laurence is the

The Knolls rely on conventional oak aging of their wines

youngest, an attractive young Frenchwoman, a self-confident Alsatian, multi-lingual and a trained enologist with experience from abroad, and she is responsible for the vineyard and the cellar.

"One needs many harmonious factors for a great Riesling, but a good terroir is a prerequisite, since Riesling is capable of expressing every little nuance of the soil, even in quite discriminating ways. Riesling is a personality, subtle, but also traditional and always elegant."

Laurence Faller says this with the self-confidence of a woman who knows what real elegance means. "It is the rail along which glides the vigor which is in my Rieslings, without denying its bodily-rich structure, nor appearing ponderous, perhaps, rather, playfully

Baroque." In this sense, the young enologist accepts botrytis: "I just love a little botrytis in Riesling, that gives it this inimitable depth in its aroma. No other variety in the world can do this." Laurence Faller relies on biodynamic cultivation, the introduction of wild yeasts and large, old oak vats. She harvests her various Rieslings from the parcels of land of the granite-rocky grand cru Schlossberg site as late as possible so that the aromatic vigor of the grapes is concentrated, and later expresses in the glass what has made the Fallers well-known far beyond the borders of quiet Alsace: very expressive Rieslings with stature, finesse, vigor and elegance, that have endured over the years and which embody traditional monuments of Alsatian Riesling culture.

NOBLE
SWEETNESS
Riesling's crowning achievement

Sweetness, which is usually equated with sugar, is encumbered by the image of heaviness, sluggishness and of something that makes you fat. Even today, these attributes are also transferred to Riesling, since unfortunately time and again winemakers concealed the flavor weaknesses of the wine with residual sugar. In the 1970s and 80s, Riesling lost its worldwide fame and the botrytized Riesling lost its renown of a unique, flavor experience – above all in Germany and Austria – as a result of the wave of simple, cheap, sweet wines.

In this category however, we are concerned with sweet Rieslings which, with the adjunct "edel" (noble), have achieved a true knightly accolade – Rieslings whose whole idea is sweetness. The obvious strengths of these, as a rule, very slowly fermented wines arise from the enormous arc of tension created by the strongly-packed sweetness and delicious fruit aromas in connection with a very lively acidity. In comparison with most other sweet wines around the world, botrytized Rieslings make do on the one hand with very low alcohol levels, sometimes only 6.5% vol., and on the other without oak barrels. In the bouquet, a tender, honey-like scent can be perceived, which is less reminiscent of sugar, but more of very ripe and concentrated fruit aromas like apricot, apple, mango and pineapple. Thanks to their high viscosity, the wines come across on the palate as very thick and sometimes a

little sticky, but nevertheless without losing their seductive fruity-sweet suppleness which holds together the honey-like and exotically multilayered fruit aromas.

In many winegrowing regions of the world, attempts are made to produce botrytized Rieslings. But Riesling only produces the real classics in Germany. In this concentration of fruit, they are obviously the specialty of northern cultivation regions and are thus an incarnation of all that Riesling grapes can offer in flavor intensity. Botrytized Rieslings are real treasures of wine culture and are among the longest-lived wines of all.

CONCENTRATING ON THE ESSENTIALS

Botrytized Rieslings are obtained from overripe grapes naturally shriveled on the vine. The pacemaker of this phenomenon is the fungus *Botrytis cinerea*. It perforates the grape skin, the juice evaporates and the grapes become raisin-like and shrivel up more and more. The subsequent loss of fluid results in the desired concentration of sugar and acidity in the grape. For the winemaker, this is a very delicate high-wire act between the desired, positive noble rot and the negative gray rot, which releases unpleasant aromas. The grape selection needed here, which may include the selection of individual grapes where necessary, requires an enormous expenditure of manual labor; thus only small amounts can be produced. In addition there is the risk of inclement weather: in the case of continual rainfall or early frost, the rotting process may be negatively influenced.

QUALITATIVE SWEETNESS

The greater the sweetness in Riesling, the higher also the grade of the botrytized wine, which in Germany and Austria is graded into Auslese, Beerenauslese, Trockenbeerenauslese and Eiswein (ice wine), and in Alsace is produced as Sélection des grains nobles. In addition there are the ice wine variations, which in the USA and Canada are designated as such. Within this spectrum, ranging from Auslese to ice wine, each level is clearly defined. According to the German wine laws of 1971, the Auslese quality in Germany unfortunately no longer has a clear flavoral profile; today it is developed in a dry style by winemakers as well as in the botrytized form. Traditionally, naturally-sweet Rieslings from overripe or botrytized grapes which were selectively picked, were designated as Auslese.

The Alsatian Sélection des grains nobles roughly corresponds to this rating and with a must weight of at least 110° Oechsle, it is placed clearly above the late-harvested Vendange tardive (Spätlese).

A level of 110° to 128° Oechsle – depending on the growing area – is required by a Beerenauslese. Here also – as the name Beerenauslese (grape selection) suggests – overripe portions of bunches affected by noble rot are individually selected. A Riesling-Beerenauslese is an extremely intensively-sweet wine with a scent of raisins and dried fruit. The enormously high aroma concentration forms the essence and produces compact Rieslings with elegant acidity, fine honey-sweetness and great po-

tential for development. The rare Trockenbeerenauslese is produced from raisin-like shriveled grapes and is an extremely thick, intensive and complex wine with a delicate acidity structure and an aging potential of many decades. Even here, the process of selection is absolutely essential. Without a doubt, these Rieslings are among the most expensive white wines in the world.

HOT LOVE FOR ICE WINE

Ice wines are particular rarities which are obtained in severe frost. In contrast to other botrytized wines such as those of Auslese, Beerenauslese and Trockenbeerenauslese qualities, the secret of ice wines is in the harvesting of frozen grapes. They may be picked at a temperature of -7°C or below, ideally at -10 to -12°C. The naturally frozen grapes are immediately pressed in this "icy" state. The water in the grapes is left behind as ice in the press, while only the sweetest juice – whose freezing point is lower than that of water – is obtained as a highly concentrated must. There is not much more to be pressed out of the frozen grapes, quality is set above quantity. With scrupulous exactness, passionate ice-wine makers ensure a healthy yield of grapes unaffected by botrytis. Indeed, a great ice wine requires above all healthy grapes as source material, and exactly herein lies the difference between the botrytized growths such as Beerenauslese and Trockenbeerenauslese. A high-class ice wine does not exhibit the flavoral characteristics of noble rot. A healthy grape yield ensures much more of an incomparably concentrated, fresh-fruity flavor and in association with the relatively high acidity, it brings about an explosively flavoral tension.

Egon Müller

Weingut Egon Müller-Scharzhof

Legends have something fascinating about them, and the Scharzhof estate on the Saar is no exception. For generations, the Müllers have defined the talents of Riesling on the slopes of the famous Scharzhofberg, whose predestined site was already recognized by the Romans, and for generations the name Egon has been passed down to sons of the family. A tradition that is as certain as the exceptional quality of their Rieslings. Those who have ever drunk a botrytized Riesling from Egon Müller were able to look the variety "deep into its eyes" and recognize its real grandeur, and more than ever its potential.

"In 1989, the last dry Spätlese wine appeared on the estate. Neither my father nor our head wine-maker nor I enjoyed the dry wines from the Scharzhofberg. Our passion is the botrytized Ries-lings, this unique combination of elegance and sweetness, which needs to be wrested from na-ture. An Auslese wine must be made from select-ed botrytized grapes, this gives rise to an addi-tional component, a higher level of the wines and an exceptional complexity. For me however, it's not the ice wines but the Beerenauslese and Trockenbeerenauslese wines which are the great-est challenge, and one requires a truly great vine-yard, a great vintage and many years of ex-perience. With regard to nature, the winemaker must assert himself, such qualities are not simply given away. Nature will not grant it of its own accord, and it becomes clear that one has creat-ed something. Naturally, hard work is necessary for all exceptional qualities, even if the relatively cool Scharzhofberg with its deep slaty soil offers first-class conditions. And there is always a little trepidation as to whether the wine will taste of the Scharzhofberg."

Egon Müller speaks of the Scharzhofberg as if it were a personality that one cherishes and loves, and always accompanies at a healthy distance, for familiarity breeds contempt. "If while sampling the young wines, we find both herbs and slate, then everything is okay. Then it will be a Scharzhofberger which retains the character of its place of origin even after decades," says Egon Müller who, along with the more common foreign languages, also speaks fluent Japanese, and who enthuses over the 1976-vintage Scharzhofberger Riesling Auslese wine in a manner that creates a desire for more.

Ernst Loosen

Weingut Dr. Loosen

When Ernst Loosen talks with grand gestures of his first experiences of wine sales in Eng-land, then he has to grin: "Fine, sweet Ries-lings from the Mosel? Not interested!" was the continual answer. Ernst Loosen, at that time a student at the college in Geisenheim, did not allow himself to be disheartened by such setbacks. "Many dealers had no particu-lar conception of a Mosel Riesling at all, and this must definitely be reestablished! This was obvious to me back then." Indeed, for the winegrower Ernst Loosen, Riesling counts as one of the great varieties worldwide, as one of the very greatest. And he says this not simply because his Rieslings already belong to the top category. Loosen is not restricted to a local, provincial thinking, he is interested in all wines of this world. There is hardly a country or a variety that he does not know, or about

The Rieslings of Ernst Loosen enjoy a worldwide reputation

conditions and at the same time introduces minerality into the Rieslings. A unique soil which does not initially need to be rediscovered in terroir discussions. It is simply there, and therein lies the typical."

He consistently transforms the potential of his vineyards – which are located in world-famous sites such as the Wehlener Sonnenuhr, Ürziger Würzgarten and the Erdener Prälat – into remarkable quality in all of his Riesling wines. But his botrytized specialties, above all the Goldkapsel Auslese wine, make the taste buds really pulsate. "The Goldkapsel wine always has a small amount of botrytis, this puts an edge on the aroma, and after aging, the wines appear somewhat more opulent, thanks to honey-notes," he explains. The wine speaks for itself. "It's pleasing to be able to appreciate the soil," he says after the first sip, "the finesse of the slate is unmistakable." Every site is typically, and above all individually, tastable, even the ancients said this. But it is typical however also for Ernst Loosen, whose wines are in demand all around the world, today more that ever.

which he cannot discuss. For this reason particularly, he is convinced about terroir-oriented natural wine concepts and he has a quite specific vision for his Rieslings, that you can comprehensibly taste.
"Elegant wines that require only a little alcohol and possess a well-proportioned acidity structure: from a tender Kabinett wine of slender form, to a juicy Spätlese wine up to a complex, botrytized Riesling. Which region can offer all this in such breadth? It's perfectly clear, the Mosel!"
Ernst Loosen determinedly adds:
"Riesling must smolder by day, but cool down during the nights in order to achieve an optimal vegetation and thereby also the stature-forming delicate acidity. The dark slate soil offers these

Wilhelm Weil
WEINGUT ROBERT WEIL

"I have put my heart and soul – and my mind – into winemaking, and I am a winemaker in the Rheingau, and if you are a winemaker in the Rheingau, then you are a Riesling winemaker, both of these aspects belong inseparably together. I'm thankful for this, since Riesling is the most versatile variety in its application and can produce a magnificent palette of the most varying wines of the very highest quality. Today, thanks to considerable experience and strict quality man-

agement, we can produce great, dry Rieslings in our vineyards. This is undisputed, and yet: when the grandiose game of natural, higher concentration in the grape with the self-assured Riesling-typical acidity begins, and when, after the Auslese wine harvest, we harvest the botrytized wines still at the beginning of December, then Riesling in northern climes demonstrates its unchallenged top position among the wines of the world. Together with the Sauternes and the Tokay it has represented since ancient times the classic trio of sweet wines. In this trio it is, with all its concentration and sustainability, the elegant type, which beguiles with low alcohol and the indescribable balance of high residual sweetness and expressive acidity. Above all however, it is the great botrytized Rieslings from special vintages which will outlive us in the treasure chambers of wine estates and those which – when they are uncorked by future generations – will speak of our wine age and our wine ideas."

nary Rieslings. The spick and span, clear and fruity wines caused a stir in the wine scene. Above all, the botrytized top-quality wines took all the awards in the competitions in which they were exhibited. Still today, the Kellers' botrytized Rieslings are placed right at the front in rankings, along with the traditional classic wines of the Rheingau and the Mosel. The Kellers' son Klaus-Peter, who now manages the estate, has the great dry Rieslings rather more in his sights however, which in terms of quantity, represent the lion's share of wines on the estate. "We have advanced further in terms of flavor, and our customers have also changed as a consequence," he says, and sees the profile of the estate rather more in the dry sector. Accounting for the past? Klaus-Peter Keller has enough personal ambition to demonstrate that he can keep pace with even the great dry Rieslings.

Klaus-Peter Keller
Weingut Keller

No one knew of this family business in Dalsheim, certainly not before about 20 years ago. In the Rheinhessian hinterland, where there is otherwise no particular winegrowing tradition, it was impossible to produce top-class wines. That was the conventional wisdom at that time. Klaus and Hedwig Keller proved the critics to be wrong, and with extraordi-

Klaus-Peter Keller indisputably belongs to the German Riesling elite

With botrytized Rieslings, the Rheinhessian has long since produced evidence.

"I appreciate botrytized Rieslings and I'm also happy to drink them. It is a shame that in Germany there is so little interest in botrytized wines. Certainly, you have to explain them, which is, interestingly, not necessary abroad. On the contrary, at wine presentations, customers look at me with shining eyes and are absolutely delighted with a botrytized Riesling."

Perhaps also because it is so incomparable in this multilayered, finesse-rich cellar-quality, and thus offers an instance of heavenly Riesling-exotic which is very difficult to imitate.

Helmut Dönnhoff
Weingut Hermann Dönnhoff

Where should one begin with the Dönnhoff estate? Which wine should be tasted first, and where are comparisons to be found? We are already speaking of a legend, and it appears that Helmut Dönnhoff could bridge the remoteness that surrounds this phrase. Helmut Dönnhoff is approachable, open, a winemaker without affectations. However, his wines are not simply good. What this winemaker has been producing for years, is always something special, and he knows it. They are wines of a special brilliance.

"I am simply very pleased when one of my Rieslings tastes good, then we shall talk about why it tastes good. Riesling is my life, it signifies light, lust, zest for life. I try to realize these feelings in my wines. There is no other wine that can express itself in so many ways as Riesling can. At the same time, it resists standardization, it resists a too-strong influence of alcohol and a too-massive stature. It simply does not allow it, because then it cannot elegantly develop. That's why there's no point in defining which type is the right one, residual-sweet or dry. Both are possible, in each case one must simply let the individual site speak for itself. The Oberhausener Brücke lends itself for example to the lacy, residually sweet method of developing a wine, in its best aspect. The Niederhäuser Hermannshöhle is rather more suited to the great, dry, complex wine."

Helmut Dönnhoff is fully proficient in both styles. His residual-sweet Rieslings are already legendary, but he considers them in his own unassuming modesty.

"I do not require a Trockenbeerenauslese every year, in order to be content. Only nature itself determines this, and I have little influence on that. The winemaker must know only where he is heading, he must have the wine in his head. To

**His Rieslings are in demand worldwide:
Helmut Dönnhoff**

The south-facing vineyard slopes of the Escherndorfer Lump site guarantee ideal sunshine

work against nature is in any case far too expensive. I nevertheless find it fascinating that grapes which have grown in cool climates taste like fruits which come from equatorial regions."
In his botrytized Rieslings, the taste of the fruit aromas is as crystal clear as fresh spring water.

Horst Sauer
Weingut Horst Sauer

"Fränkisch trocken" (Franconian dry) is a common term in the German wine world. It is remarkable that of all people a Franconian winemaker, and moreover one with the name of Sauer (meaning "acid"), produces fascinat-

ing botrytized wines. Horst Sauer has eked out a position among the few great botrytized-wine specialists with his extravagant Beerenauslese, Trockenbeerenauslese and ice wines. An honor that does not just appear from nowhere.

"Normally, I don't have much patience. But if the matter at hand is botrytized wines, then I have to employ an unlimited amount of patience. I must not become hectic. One has a style of wine in one's head, it's like a jigsaw puzzle that needs to be pieced together. Only when all the pieces are in place, can the delightful picture be seen. The production of great botrytized wines sometimes also requires sacrifice. When I have harvested a Beerenauslese or Trockenbeerenauslese wine and it does not measure up to my criteria, then it will not be bottled!"

Horst Sauer is consistent and self-critical. "Particularly the great Rieslings do not forgive any compromising." The botrytized grapes are fragile.

"Because of the high humidity, botrytis develops to a considerable extent on the Escherndorfer Lump. In the fall, the damp slowly rises up the hillside, and the grapes become moist. The right moment is decisive. With botrytized-wines, one must work very quickly, to begin the fermentation as soon as possible after pressing, and only then is it possible to take more time. All our Rieslings are developed in stainless steel containers. The difficulty is to find the exact moment at which fermentation should cease. The best situation is when the Rieslings' fermentation stops automatically and their representative character is effectively self-determining. It is important that the balance between sweetness, acidity and alcohol is achieved."

Ulrich Mell is master of the entire Riesling repertoire, from dry to botrytized wines

Ulrich Mell
Weingut Geheimer Rat
Dr. von Bassermann-Jordan

"Geheimer Rat Dr. von Bassermann-Jordan" not only sounds like tradition: this Pfalz estate founded in 1718 is also one of the great monuments of German wine culture. In contrast, Uli Mell sounds, in a nutshell, quite refreshing and dynamic. Both together – Bassermann and Mell – it is a concept promising success. Indeed, together with the general manager Gunther Hauck, Mell has put this monument to the history of German wine back on track. Chief winemaker Ulrich Mell proceeds cautiously, even with his Rieslings. After all, the variety has a proportion of about 90% on the Bassermann-Jordan estate. The sites in which the Rieslings grow are among the best in the region: Forster Ungeheuer, Forster Pechstein, Forster Jesuitengarten and Forster Kirchenstück. In addition, Deidesheimer Hohenmorgen and Deidesheimer Kieselberg. An ideal initial situation, and Ulrich Mell takes this chance, since he is part of a great tradition. The majority of Rieslings are developed dry in the Kabinett and Spätlese range, but at the same time, the estate has been the botrytized wine-figurehead of the Pfalz region for nearly 200 years.

In 1811, the first botrytized Riesling was produced on the Deidesheimer estate, one of the truly great vintages. With this monument Bassermann-Jordan was added to the list of the top producers of botrytized wines which, until then were primarily in the Rheingau and Mosel regions. Mell's botrytized Rieslings are small works of art, a harmonic string of complex fruit aromas, that fit together as if they were made for each other. The heartily refreshing acidity dances with the sweet aromas and at the same time reins them in so that the flavoral harmony remains steady. It is Ulrich Mell's talent that consigns these contradictory components into a wine and thereby to retain the right balance. Elegantly made. Botrytized Riesling in one batch.

Olivier Humbrecht
ZIND-HUMBRECHT

The Alsace has its checkered history between Germany and France to thank for a wine culture with styles which are resident between the two nations. Vendange tardive and Sélection des grains nobles correspond to the German designations of Auslese and Beerenauslese / Trockenbeerenauslese, and are produced with perfection by a number of winemakers between Strasbourg and Colmar. Olivier Humbrecht is one of these great perfectionists. Not only is this stately winemaker well over 6 feet tall, but the renowned Zind-Humbrecht estate in the tiny, medieval village of Turckheim is one of the businesses in Alsace which, along with great dry wine qualities, also produces botrytized specialties of particular excellence. Olivier Humbrecht, who furthermore holds the title of Master of Wine, manages the business with vision and skill. He has long since adapted to biodynamic cultivation and allows only a restrained treatment of his wines during the various processes in the cellar. He offers Rieslings in a number of variations: "It is the most elegant white wine in the world", he says, "when the harvest yield is of impeccable quality and ripeness." His Sélections des grains nobles certainly impress with a delicate complexity and finesse, which only a few winemakers worldwide can accomplish in this elegance.

Karl Kaiser
INNISKILLIN

The somewhat curious name of the estate originates not from a rare Austrian dialect, but can be traced back to an Irish regiment of fusiliers stationed in North America in 1812. In contrast, Karl Kaiser is a real Austrian who has lived in Canada for over thirty years, and has fulfilled a dream here. In 1975, he founded Inniskillin Wines in Niagara-on-the-Lake, together with Donald Ziraldo. It was the first winery license in Ontario since 1929. Karl Kaiser's vision to make exceptionally good wines from selected grapes, naturally then allowed him to experiment with ice wine as well.

"I love this powerful intensity of the tropical fruit aromas that can be obtained from the frozen grapes, the intensive feeling on the palate, this sensational encounter with clear fruit, fine sweetness and fresh acidity, that will remain long in one's memory. These are the wines which arise from our soil and our climate and which can be readily presented to the world of wine."

In 1991, a 1989 Inniskillin ice wine was awarded the "Grand Prix d'Honneur" in Bordeaux. As a result, with Austrian help, Canada entered into the annals of this specialty. A few years after this triumph, Inniskillin was gobbled up by the American wine giant Vincor International.

CHAPTER 5

TELL ME THE WAY TO RIESLING

FROM CORRECT HANDLING, TO THE BEST ADDRESSES

THE RIGHT PERSPECTIVE

The glass world of Riesling

The glass is an important instrument in order to be able to enjoy wine in all its facets. However, before entering the world of glass, one should know how taste functions. Although generally, one speaks of "taste" when eating and drinking, the sense of smell plays a large part in the perception. Since the oral cavity is connected to the olfactory nerves via the pharynx, tasting and smelling take place at the same time.

The tongue alone can differentiate between only four flavors. Sweetness is perceived at the tip of the tongue, taste receptors that recognize bitterness are located at the back of the tongue, and the edges of the tongue perceive the salty and the sour.

Before the actual taste arises, the tongue feels out the temperature and the viscosity – whether oily or fluid. Now then, don't slacken! To swallow the wine immediately would shorten the pleasure. This is why the wine is moved around the mouth, in order to address all taste receptors. Some wine tasters purse their lips, in order to suck in an additional draft of air to be mixed with the wine and thereby to experience the flavor more intensively.

GLASS DISCIPLINE

To have the right glass for Riesling is not a necessity, but it is advisable. Today, the selection of glasses on the market is enormous, and with the aim of making a choice easier, certain principles should be adhered to: Colored glasses belong in the display cabinet. A wine glass should on principle be colorlessly clear. Even cut crystal can interfere with the evaluation of color brilliance.

The color of the glass however has no effect at all upon the flavor of the wine. In contrast, the form of the glass, its thickness and its rim determine how the wine falls upon the tongue and its taste zones. Nevertheless, as an instrument of tasting, the glass cannot perform miracles. The requirement for a differentiated perception of the wine is ultimately the quality of the wine itself.

LONG STEMS

Glasses with long stems are more efficiently manipulated because they avoid unattractive finger prints on the bowl and thereby also avoid an increase in the temperature of the wine through warmth from the hand. The bowl should also taper towards the top, and allow ample space for the wine so that it does not spill out with the first rotating of the glass. For this same reason, wine glasses should only be filled to one third, or a maximum of half-full. By careful rotation, the evaporation surface is increased, the diversity of the aromas develop more rapidly, and the aroma molecules can rise up more easily and be perceived more intensively.

TYPES OF GLASS AND RIESLING CATEGORIES

Fruit, acidity, tannins and alcohol are the variable wine components whose perception can be conveyed and influenced via the glass. This is why the choice of the right glass is decisive, in order to perceive the balance and the harmonious relationship of the individual elements of the wine to one another. Thus, the flavoral image of a note of bitterness can be variously sensed, depending on the type of glass: from agreeably rounded, with a fruit underlay, to grassy, green or even disagreeably medicinal.

A single glass that satisfies all requirements does not exist. This is why it is necessary to compromise. A multifunctional, universally-applicable all-rounder would be quite practical, one which would altogether come closest to the above-mentioned characteristics. That would not simply be the financially favorable variant, but also a space-saving alternative. However, it is a simple fact that Rieslings in particular better, and above all more clearly, demonstrate the distinctive individuality of their varying styles in correspondingly appropriate glasses.

The absolutely essential basic equipment includes the right glass

Sound basis

For Rieslings of the "sound basis" category, the all-rounder described above is most favorably suited. These palatable bread-and-butter Rieslings for day-to-day use go well with the all-rounder, because the glass enhances the intensive aroma typical of the Riesling variety. The balance of fruit and acidity comes into its own.

Delicate finesse

Additionally, the delicate, finesse-rich Kabinett wines are appropriately comfortable in the all-rounder. However, they develop more delicately and finely in a mouth-blown glass of similar form. On the other hand, a tulip-shaped glass with a rim that is slightly curved outward allows the acidity of these light wines to emerge too strongly.

Fruity diversity

This also applies to the diverse fruit of a multifaceted, fruity-sweet Spätlese wine type. According to the volume and ripeness, a somewhat more bulging glass would certainly benefit the wine by capturing the wonderful aromas and passing them, more compressed, towards the nose.

Complex elegance

As a rule, complex, elegant Rieslings possess an intensive aroma of peach and apricot that is typical of the variety, and in addition a high amount of minerality. They correspondingly contain extracts and alcohol levels between 12

and 13% vol. and usually a powerful acidity. All this requires a fine glass with a relatively high "chimney" – the space above the wine in the glass – and a surface that is not too large, so that the wine does not appear too alcoholic. In this way the Riesling gains in elegance and its complex multilayered aspect is harmoniously perceived on the palate.

Baroque monuments

As a rule, these vigorous, often luscious Rieslings love large, bulging glasses in which they can fully develop and give voice to their entire aroma spectrum. A Pinot Noir glass may be employed here as well. It can be used for daily needs and for spicy, creamy Smaragd-Veltliner wines as well as for vigorous, oak-aged Chardonnays. An opulent Riesling can be best shown to advantage in a glass with a large diameter because the surface of the wine receives sufficient contact with the air.

Noble sweetness

Their extreme density and high concentration of aromas allow botrytized, multifaceted Rieslings to get away with smaller goblets. However, it is important for the aroma as well as for the later impression of taste to develop in ideal fashion, and this is why it makes sense to utilize mouth-blown glasses, because they accentuate the fine aromas especially well. The fruit acidity of the sweet Riesling may be a little intensified on the palate. Thus, a flavoral harmony occurs, and the delicate combination of intensive fruit, stimulating acidity and delightful sweetness can come to the fore.

Mineral water is an ideal accompaniment to Rieslings of all styles

BASIC
ACCOUTERMENTS

Riesling basics for drinking pleasure

Enjoying wines need not be expensive. Proper wine glasses are part of the minimum of basic equipment, because they are the most important instruments for correctly evaluating color, aromas and flavor. It is of course possible to extract the cork from the bottle's neck with most basic corkscrews, however, we recommend a proper waiter's knife. In addition, there is an almost unlimited offer of useful and useless accessories to suit every pocket.

TAKING AIR

Decanting wine is not a magic trick for improving quality, but a common method of separating solid particles from the liquid. In most cases it is a question of the so-called deposit in the bottle, which unpleasantly grates between the teeth, and should therefore be removed from the wine. For this reason the bottle is carefully opened and slowly poured into a decanter under the light of a candle or a lamp. The light shows up the opaque and suspended particles which preferably should not reach the bottle's neck and are thus also kept out of the decanter. The wine in the decanter is now clear, and preferably only a small quantity remains in the bottle containing the entire deposit. Another reason for decanting can be the intended aerating of the wine. Because of the oxygen influence while transferring the wine from the bottle to the decanter, hard, severe and above all young wines – white as well as red – become rounder and more expressive in flavor. The longer the time between decanting and serving, the stronger will be the effect of aeration, and incidentally, with almost all wines decanting leads to a flavoral improvement, perhaps with the exception of mature Pinots Noirs (Spätburgunder).

ADVISABLE

Good advice need not be expensive. However, with the vast range of wines on offer, it is worthwhile seeking advice from specialist wine dealers, and as a rule, their selection, service, knowledge of wine and their prices tally. Even where it is necessary to invest just a little more than in the supermarket, sound advice can be obtained from vintners, and talking to experienced dealers can lead to further developments in one's understanding of wine. Very important is the fact that the best wine is the one that tastes best. A good wine which you like, cannot therefore be too expensive. A wine that does not taste good to you is, however, always too expensive!

WINE-RACK AND RUIN

Wines alter with time – sometimes positively, sometimes not. It could be that a number of cases of a particular wine is immediately purchased in a fit of post-tasting enthusiasm, and they are placed in the cellar, but after two or three years it is found that it tastes rather flat and dull, or even unpleasant. There can be two reasons for this: Either the wine was a "deceiver" which had no aging capacity, or perhaps storage conditions were not suitable. The straightforward, inexpensive, everyday Riesling is best consumed soon after purchase. High-quality Rieslings may be given some more time, and they can develop positively. This also applies to complex, dry Rieslings as well as for all botrytized specialties, which usually possess ageing potential for decades. The winemaker or the wine dealer should be able to give competent advice on whether a wine is suitable for storage and above all for how long.

You can however, always consider the following basic principles: a Riesling that is bitter in its youth will not lose this note even after decades. Bitterness suggests green, unripe phenols which become rather more aggressive with increasing age. A dry Riesling with a lot of acidity only develops ideally when the acidity is buffered with extracts, alcohol or residual sugar. There would otherwise be the risk of the wine "drying out" and later presenting less acidity but also an empty flavor.

TEMPERATURE

There are no generally valid rules regarding how warm or cold a wine should be. Ultimately, all individuals have their own conception of temperature, and it is simply a matter of individual feeling. As with the conception of smells and taste, temperature is also a matter of a sensory impression, which can vary with atmospheric conditions, external and internal temperatures and above all personal mood. In winter, higher temperatures are preferred, whereas in summer cooler drinks are generally in demand, but what really matters is simply what tastes good!

Serving or drinking?

When talking of an ideal wine temperature, the difference between serving and drinking temperature must be taken into account. Thus, for example the warmth of a room has a clearly apparent influence on the serving temperature, and in a well-filled restaurant with an average room temperature, a cooled Riesling can be warmed by two to three degrees within only a few minutes. Thicker glasses can additionally accelerate this process, especially if they are taken, still warm, directly out of the dishwasher, or if they are kept in a relatively warm place. Transferring the wine to a decanting carafe also warms the wine by at least 1 to 2 °C.

Cooled Riesling

Today more than ever before, wines are offered which are designed for immediate or prompt consumption. From the supermarket shelf, into the refrigerator and a few hours later it's on the table – this is no problem. It is not necessary to recreate a complicated vaulted cellar, simple everyday wines easily endure a few days and weeks in the refrigerator. If the wine is stored in the relatively warm cellar of an average family house, and on occasion it needs to be rapidly cooled, there is no objection to putting the Riesling in the freezer compartment, or quickly cooling it down with a Rapid Ice wine chiller sleeve. This method is certainly better than drinking the wine too warm and thereby missing out on the enjoyment of it.

Careful with the aged

Mature, high-quality Rieslings are however distinctly more fragile in their structure. They should be very carefully brought to the right temperature. The cold retards the development of the aromas, and this means a loss in flavor. A word of advice: Champagne coolers with ice cubes are taboo for such Rieslings, because they bring the wine near to freezing point and thereby deprive it of any kind of aromatic interplay.

Which temperature for which Riesling type?

By contrast however, Rieslings of the "sound basis" category are wonderfully suited to cool temperatures. They may be taken from the refrigerator and poured directly into the glass. This harms neither the typical aroma of the variety nor the luscious acidity. These uncomplicated Rieslings should not be drunk too warm, otherwise they lose their thrill.

Kabinett wines of the "delicate finesse" type likewise love cool temperatures; however, they can endure somewhat higher temperatures thanks to their relatively low alcohol content. Since they have within them a harmonious combination of fruit, acidity, sweetness and alcohol, they can be served between 7 and 10°C quite according to preference. The exact temperature can only be determined with a thermometer, but preferably, one should rely on discerning the temperature by feel. That is why the old rule of thumb is used: when in doubt, the wine should be served rather on the colder side than on the warmer, since it will become warm itself.

In their youth, when the fruit aromas still noticeably prevail, multifaceted, fruit-sweet Spätlese wines react similarly to Kabinett wines. In a more mature condition however, one should allow them a more moderate temperature of 10 to 12°C. They are grateful for it and display decidedly more from their flavoral spectrum.

Grand cru wines in the dry flavoral style, but also opulent, mature Rieslings should not be drunk too warm. Their usually high alcohol levels, which can certainly reach between 12 and 14% vol., would otherwise develop broad, unpleasant notes and take away the sustaining elegance. So that they can exhibit their immense multilayered aspect along with their vigor, they should be drunk between 10 and 13°C.

Auslese, Beerenauslese, Trockenbeerenauslese and ice wines distinguish themselves through their delicate combination of exciting acidity and fruit-sweetness. They should never be drunk too warm, since then the acidity falls away and the corresponding sweetness can appear sticky and ponderous.

ELECTIVE AFFINITIES

Riesling and eating

Wine simply belongs to a lifestyle rich in pleasures, so it should accompany food in any case, and not only on festive occasions. Riesling allows many pleasurable combinations that can harmoniously connect to one another – if certain principles are followed. It is not a matter of whether white wine goes with fish and red wine suits game. In order to achieve a flavoral harmony between wine and food, it comes down to the flavor-defining elements such as spices, sauces or ways of cooking and preparation methods. Is the fish grilled, poached or marinated? Was the meat cooked, grilled, fried or braised in the oven? Which herbs and spices provide aromas in addition, and which sauce has an influence upon the dish and how intensely? Because of the multifarious combination possibilities it is important to know about the interactions of the ingredients of wines and food, in order to produce combinations with the best possible flavoral effects. This can be achieved via harmonious combinations, but also through contrasting ones.

These flavors react with and augment one another: sweet and sweet, salty and salty, salty and sour, sour and sour, sour and bitter, bitter and bitter.

These flavors cover up or complement each other: sweet and salty, sweet and bitter, sweet and sour, salty and bitter.

RIESLING IS CHOOSY

Acidity and acidity augment each other, and in response Riesling pulls a sour face, almost literally, and diminishes in flavor. Salt also does not go very well with Riesling's acidity. If however, the wine brings a little residual sweetness with it, then salt and fruit-sweetness can become ideal partners. Roasting aromas arising from roasted meat or fish make it difficult above all for young, fresh Rieslings with a distinctive acidity. Mature Rieslings, by all means with a touch of residual sweetness, suit such dishes much better.

The following ingredients can be added to a recipe only in very moderate quantities. They should be included only with the help of bridging ingredients and should not be dominant at all, nor should they constitute the central part of the dish, otherwise the Riesling will have no chance. Riesling does not approve of certain combinations, reacting dismissively, tasting bitter or even sour.

Globe artichokes present too-high a bitterness, and taste metallic in combination with Riesling.

Ice cream is quite simply too cold in order to be enjoyed together with Riesling, and likewise neither the fats in the cream, nor the accompanying sweetness harmonize with Riesling.

Strawberries contain a lot of fruit acid, which clashes with the acidity of Riesling.

Coffee paralyzes the taste for a good twenty minutes. Therefore, drinking coffee and wine at the same time should be avoided.

Soused herrings cause not only Rieslings to taste metallic and sour, but all wines.

In its raw state, **fruit** has a lot of fruit-sweetness and acidity, which do not agree with the Riesling's acidity. Riesling is however very compatible with stewed fruit and chutneys.

Radishes, like raw onions and **horse radish,** are very problematical for Riesling because of the combination of bitter compounds, acidity and essential oils.

Anchovies have too much salt to be able to harmonize with Riesling.

Chocolate destroys the original Riesling flavor through its high fat and sugar content.

Spinach possesses bitter compounds, which have an almost astringent effect in the mouth. They alter the fruit and acidity structure of Riesling.

Tomatoes possess a lot of acidity. Particularly light, tender Rieslings have too little substance to compete

HARMONY OR CONTRAST

It is sometimes wise to build a bridge for the Riesling in order to adequately counteract the relatively dominant acidity and sweetness, or to so unite both that the dish becomes a flavoral experience in concert with the Riesling. Harmony between wine and food can come about for example via corresponding aromas. Try out a mature Riesling Spätlese wine with apple pie, and you will discover similar apple and honey aromas in the wine and in the pie. Alternatively, open a bottle of vigorous Alsatian Riesling to go with a light, spicy, sweet sauerkraut dish – this is a classic combination that works very well.

Even aromatic contrasts have their allure. A braised oxtail with a light, smooth sauce can certainly put up with a mature Riesling with a crisp acidity structure. The braised meat as well as the smooth sauce contain sweetness and tender caramel aromas, and thereby buffer the acidity. A residual-sweet Riesling would have no chance in such a situation, and even a vigorous, dry Riesling would develop into being downright dull in this combination.

THE SAUCE PRODUCES THE TRUE FLAVOR

All types of meat and fish, but also vegetables and side dishes too, can be refined with sauces, thereby influencing their flavor. Only with the sauce is the real excitement introduced into a dish. It is the soul of the meal and thereby a very important and defining part of the combination. Therefore, the choice of a Riesling should agree with the sauce.

The gourmet chef Harald Rüssel from Landhaus St. Urban in Naurath, in Germany's Eifel region consistently relies on the finest regional cuisine with a Mediterranean influence. As a mentor of the new German cuisine, he not only has family ties to Riesling, he uses the wine for refining his dishes und demonstrates how all component parts can be harmoniously bound together. In the gourmet scene they affectionately call him the sauce chef. Therefore, we shall use his sauces to explain here why they taste especially good, particularly in combination with Riesling.

Beurre blanc

It is one of the most important sauces in fine cooking and possesses a fine, buttery, acidic-accentuated flavor. A matured, formerly residually-sweet Kabinett wine goes well with it as does a light, matured, vigorous, complex Riesling.

Curry sauce

This variant of Beurre blanc is flavored with pieces of mango and apple, curry paste and Madras curry. The slightly hot and extremely spicy aspects of this sauce are ideally suited to fresh residual-sweet Spätlese and Auslese wines.

Pimento and ginger sauce

This is the hot variant of Beurre blanc, with ginger, chili peppers and red paprika. Thyme and rosemary as well as a stock made from lobster, crab or shrimp, provide the perfect balance with which to deglaze the sauce. The slightly hot aspect and the herbal notes make residual-sweet Rieslings of all categories ideal partners.

Morel cream

A creamy sauce that suits grand, dry Rieslings. The elegant, complex growths as well as the opulent Wachau and Alsatian Rieslings score well here. Residual-sweet Rieslings make the sauce appear rather clumsy and greasy, because the sweetness is intensified by the mushroom flavor and the cream.

Sauce bourride

This Mediterranean sauce without cream is made from fish and lobster carcasses, flavored with tomatoes and fresh bell peppers and refined with fresh herbs, orange juice and orange peel. Because of the large amount of tomatoes and bell peppers a dry Riesling tastes almost sour, while residually-sweet Kabinett and Spätlese wines can unfold their full allure, making ideal partners.

Vinaigrette

Salad with vinaigrette – vinegar and Riesling? For an appetizer, it is a virtually unresolvable culinary problem that occurs almost daily. However, if the vinaigrette is appropriate, then also the Riesling will be right. Basically, only mild vinegar should be used and the acidity of the vinegar should be softened with oil and a little tasty stock. The vinaigrette should consist of one part vinegar, one part oil and

Gourmet chef and one of the Jeunes Restaurateurs of Germany: Harald Rüssel

Suits Riesling wonderfully well: Cod with pearl barley with cured calf's head by Harald Rüssel

two parts of freshly boiled stock. The base is a preparation of shallots and various condiments, fresh sautéed vegetables, coriander, pepper and allspice, which must be left to infuse for a few hours. The flavor can be refined with mustard. The warm stock is added to the base ingredients and thickened with a little cornstarch.

Since the majority of salads are served with grilled fish, meat, terrines, hams or pâtés, they are subject to the same requirements in regard to wine as the meat or the fish of the main course. The sauce, in this case the vinaigrette, is ultimately the determining feature. If for example there is a salad with poultry, then the fried poultry liver is finely puréed and the

vinaigrette is, so to speak, scented with it. The poultry liver provides a creamy, lightly sweet-tasting texture that excellently suits Rieslings with a light residual sweetness. A neutral vegetable vinaigrette goes along with Riesling especially well. Firstly, finely diced zucchini, eggplants and carrots are lightly sautéed in a skillet and subsequently briefly chopped with an immersion blender. A natural thickening occurs, and the neutral, assuaging flavor of the vegetables ensures a compatibility with almost every type of Riesling. Also a creamy potato vinaigrette with small, diced pieces of fried bacon can pleasantly reduce the acidity in Riesling and thus become an ideal partner for dry Rieslings.

THE RIGHT ACCOMPANIMENT FOR RIESLING

Meat (pot roasted)

Roasted meat is usually served with its own creamy sauce, and thanks to the long cooking process it develops lightly sweet, caramel-like aromas. Ripe Rieslings go wonderfully well with it, and they may by all means show their own acidity.

Meat and fish (short roast)

A roast saddle of veal can be combined with Riesling without any difficulty. In such a case however, a powerful red wine sauce should be avoided and perhaps porcini with a suitable creamy sauce served in its place. If however, the fish is grilled and served with a hearty Provençal rosemary sauce, there is no Riesling in the world that can assert itself.

Herbs and spices

Almost without exception, fresh garden herbs are appropriate with all Riesling variants, since they only bolster and refine the flavor of a dish. In contrast, herbs or spices with essential oils, such as for example rosemary or sage, taste as a rule so intense that a fine Riesling flavor is noticeably consigned to the background.

Vegetables

Vegetables that possess a certain sweetness – for instance carrots, mangetout, fennel and onion – can be used in a "bridging function" in order to somewhat soften the acidity in the Riesling. Zucchini, eggplant, cucumber and kohlrabi, the so-called neutral vegetables, go well with all Riesling types. However, bitter vegetables such as radicchio and chicory should perhaps not be combined with Riesling, because they bring out its acidity too much.

Pulses

Beans, lentils and peas, but also potatoes, are a perfect accompaniment and also have a "bridging function" since they contain starch and can therefore bind acidity or roast aromas.

Riesling and cheese

Riesling is not really an ideal wine for cheeses, but there are combinations that are mutually suited and that taste good, for example fresh goats' cheese with a fresh, young Riesling with moderate acidity. In contrast, strong cheese from cows' milk with sticky reddish-orange rind washed in saltwater brine – such as Muenster, Ami Chambertin and Époisses – prefer ripe Spätlese or Auslese wines. On the other hand, all noble and sweet Rieslings go well with blue mold cheese. The Riesling should however have volume. A tender Mosel Spätlese wine would be positively smothered by the high salt content, while Beerenauslese and Trockenbeerenauslese wines would constitute a marvelous combination.

Riesling and "Asian cuisine"

"There is no such thing as 'Asian' cuisine any more than there is a uniform 'European' cuisine." This is an unambiguous assertion by Kazuya Fukuhira, who has lived and worked in Germany for many years. His real love is for Rheingau Riesling. He therefore knows how to handle the classic combination pitfalls of this very individual variety, and he is also in command of the splendid highlights that Riesling can offer in connection with exotic Asian aromas. Under the heading "Asia" one thinks above all of exotic spices, herbs, fruit and vegetables from various countries in Asia as well as their wealth of expression in all their combinations and various cooking techniques from the very varied cuisines from Japan, China, Vietnam, Thailand and Indonesia. Unlike most European cooking styles, almost all Asian cuisine styles rely on the dominance of spices and special aromas. Salt is seldom used, and the salty flavor is achieved with special marinades as well as with salty fish and soy sauces. However, infernally hot curry pastes, tandoori, hot wasabi (Japanese horseradish) und extremely sweet sauces are used, for example a teriyaki marinade with sugar and rice wine.

The delight of many Asian dishes is due to the aromatic contrast between spicy-hot and sweet. In curried chicken with chili, coriander, ginger, lemon grass and coconut, the combination of the hot and the spicy initially dominates. The coconut milk elegantly softens the hot aspect, and thanks to its fat content, it pushes the spicy and herbal aromas to the fore.

Likewise, the aromatic Riesling corresponds ideally with the piquant spices of many Asian cooking styles: particularly Rieslings with a distinctive fruit, fine residual sweetness, delicate acidity and low alcohol are the ideal accompaniment to dominantly spicy, somewhat hot and sometimes salty aromas, because they perfectly balance the expressive flavor with their multilayered aspect, and sustain the dish as a fresh, invigorating element. A Riesling with high residual sweetness loses the dominant, sweet flavor, presents itself as being rather more refreshing and fruity, yet supple,

A master of the Asian and European culinary arts: Kazuya Fukuhira

and accordingly the hot aspect of the dish is considerably downplayed. The hot aspect drains, as it were, into the sweetness of the Riesling. A dry, complex Riesling would not stand a chance, the wine would taste even drier, and the fruit and all finesse, and above all the suppleness would be taken from it. The same can be said for salty influences. A Riesling with residual sweetness on the other hand, would superbly balance these components.

SPARKLING RIESLING

Tingling aromas under pressure

Sparkling hock, as it is known in the English-speaking world, or what the Germans call "Sekt", may be made from Riesling grapes, and most Riesling winemakers have it on offer. However, of the sparkling wines made from Riesling grapes, by no means all really sparkle. By contrast, winemakers who do not see their sparkling wines simply as a secondary use for mediocre grape material produce high-class, quality products in their own right with recognizable Riesling-typicity. Bernhard Kirsten from Klüsserath is one of the specialists for sparkling Riesling wines. He knows that the correct approach to sparkling wines is with the same quality criteria as with an ambitious wine.

Thus the trend is clearly in the direction of high-class sparkling wines made with classic, traditional bottle fermentation, which possess well-integrated carbonation and finesse and in which the character of the variety is recognizable. Ideal guidelines for Riesling, which remains true to itself during the sparkling winemaking and which alters its typical flavor considerably less than other varieties.

In their tingling condition, sparkling Riesling wines very consistently present the aromas that were at hand in the base wine. "Above all, the requirements are ripe and healthy grapes in Spätlese wine quality, since even small proportions of a botrytized batch can negatively affect the freshness during the aging process and introduce slightly bitter and petroleum tones into the sparkling wines," says Bernhard Kirsten, whose sparkling Rieslings are among the best. "The quality of the base wine is the decisive criterion for a good, sparkling Riesling."

Bernhard Kirsten produces sparkling Riesling using the traditional bottle fermentation method

ALL FROM ONE VINTAGE

In contrast to many champagnes or well known brands of sparkling hock, the majority of winemakers' sparkling Riesling wines are not based on the cuvée principle, whereby a number of wines from various vintages are blended. Rather, the trick is to produce a harmonious and balanced base wine, not too alcoholic, a process that has to begin in the vineyard. Before the wine is bottled, a mixture of wine, sugar and specially developed yeasts is introduced to initiate a second fermentation. The wine lies on the lees for between nine months and five years, which keeps it fresh and bestows it with the typical, creamy yeast flavor. When maturation comes to an end, the bottles are placed upside-down in a so-called riddling rack and each day they are riddled (turned and shaken) a little so that the yeast lees are loosened and slowly sink down into the bottle's neck. In order to remove the lees thus collected in the neck (a process known as disgorgement), the bottle necks are shock-cooled in an ice tank. When opened, the frozen lees shoot out of the bottle under pressure of the carbonation. Before the bottle is once again sealed, the loss of liquid is made up with what is known as the dosage (a high-quality wine in which, depending on the flavor, a little sugar syrup and sulfur dioxide may be dissolved).

Most sparkling Riesling wines are vinified in a "brut" (dry) flavor. There are however, also sparkling wines which, after lying on the lees, present themselves so perfectly and creamily that they require no dosage at all. They are topped up with the same sparkling wine from another bottle, and arrive as "zero dosage" on the market.

RECOMMENDED ADDRESSES

Weingut Kirsten
Krainstrasse 5, 54340 Klüsserath/Mosel
Telephone +49 6507 99115
mail@weingut-kirsten.de
www.weingut-kirsten.de

Weingut Ratzenberger
Blücherstrasse 167, 55422 Bacharach
Telephone +49 5743 1337
weingut-ratzenberger@t-online.de
www.weingut-ratzenberger.de

Sekthaus Solter
Zum Niederwald-Denkmal 2
65385 Rüdesheim am Rhein
Telephone +49 6722 2566
mail@sekthaus-solter.de
www.sekthaus-solter.de

Schloss Vaux
Kiedricher Strasse 18a
65343 Eltville am Rhein
Telephone +49 6123 62060
info@schloss-vaux.de
www.schloss-vaux.de

Sekthaus Raumland
Alzeyer Strasse 134
67592 Flörsheim-Dalsheim
Telephone +49 6243 908070
raumland@t-online.de; www.raumland.de

Wein- und Sektgut Wilhelmshof
Queichstrasse 1, 76833 Siebeldingen
Telephone +49 6345 919147
mail@wilhelmshof.de
www.wilhelmshof.de

ADDRESSES

The way to Riesling

Icons
Ⓑ Ⓓ Ⓔ Ⓕ Ⓜ Ⓢ

On the basis of six differing categories in the preceding chapters we have set up a classification according to flavor types and in each of these categories we have introduced exemplary Rieslings of particularly full character, and their winemakers. There are however, a large number of other exceptional Rieslings worldwide which nevertheless do not so readily and easily fit into our flavor-type constraints. For this reason, in the following list of addresses we have therefore used our corresponding icons only sparingly.

GERMANY

AHR

**Winzergenossenschaft
Mayschoss-Altenahr e.G.**
Ⓑ Ⓢ
Ahrrotweinstrasse 42
D-53508 Mayschoss
Telephone +49 2643 93600
wmayschoss@t-online.de
www.winzergenossenschaft-
mayschoss.de
(see page 101)

**Weingut Deutzerhof
Cossmann-Hehle**
D-53508 Mayschoss
Telephone +49 2643 7264
info@weingut-deutzerhof.de
www.weingut-deutzerhof.de

BADEN

Andreas Laible
Ⓔ
Am Bühl 6
D-77770 Durbach
Telephone +49 781 41238
info@weingut-laible.de
www.weingut-laible.de
(see page 126)

Schloss Neuweier
Mauerbergstrasse 21
D-76534 Baden-Baden
Telephone +49 7223 96670
kontakt@weingut-schloss-
neuweier.de
www.weingut-schloss-neuweier.de

Stigler
Bachenstrasse 29
D-79241 Ihringen
Telephone +49 7668 297
info@weingut-stigler.de
www.weingut-stigler.de

Achim Jähnisch
Hofmattenweg 19
D-79238 Kirchhofen
Telephone +49 7633 801161
a.jaehnisch@t-online.de
www.weingut-jaehnisch.de

Gut Nägelsförst
Ⓑ
Nägelsförst 1
D-76534 Baden-Baden
Telephone +49 7221 35550
info@naegelsfoerst.de
www.naegelsfoerst.de

Weingut Dr. Heger
Bachenstrasse 19/21
D-79241 Ihringen
Telephone +49 7668 205
info@heger-weine.de
www.heger-weine.de

FRANKEN

**Weingut am Stein
Ludwig Knoll**
Mittlerer Steinbergweg 5
D-97080 Würzburg
Telephone +49 931 25808
mail@weingut-am-stein.de
www.weingut-am-stein.de

Bickel-Stumpf
Ⓑ
Kirchgasse 5
D-97252 Frickenhausen am Main
Telephone +49 9331 2847
info@bickel-stumpf.de
www.bickel-stumpf.de

Ⓑ A sound basis   Ⓓ Fruity diversity   Ⓔ Complex elegance   Ⓕ Delicate finesse   Ⓜ Baroque monuments   Ⓢ Noble sweetness

Bürgerspital zum Hl. Geist
Theaterstrasse 19
D-97070 Würzburg
Telephone +49 931 35030
info@buergerspital.de
www.buergerspital.de

Rudolf Fürst
Hohenlindenweg 46
D-63927 Bürgstadt am Main
Telephone +49 9371 8642
info@weingut-rudolf-fuerst.de
www.weingut-rudolf-fuerst.de

Weingut Hofmann
Strüther Strasse 7
D-97285 Röttingen
Telephone +49 9338 1577
weingut.a.hofmann@t-online.de

Fürst Löwenstein
Ⓜ
Rathausgasse 5
D-97892 Kreuzwertheim
Telephone +49 9342 92350
kreuzwertheim@loewenstein.de
www.loewenstein.de
(see page 135)

Horst Sauer
Ⓑ Ⓢ
Bocksbeutelstrasse 14
D-97332 Escherndorf
Telephone +49 9381 4364
info@weingut-horst-sauer.de
www.weingut-horst-sauer.de
(see page 147)

Staatlicher Hofkeller Würzburg
Rosenbachpalais
Residenzplatz 3
D-97070 Würzburg
Telephone +49 931 3050923
hofkeller@lwg.bayern.de
www.hofkeller.de

Hans Wirsching
Ludwigstrasse 16
D-97346 Iphofen
Telephone +49 9323 87330
wirsching@t-online.de
www.wirsching.de

Schmitt's Kinder
Am Sonnenstuhl
D-97236 Randersacker
Telephone +49 931 7059197
info@schmitts-kinder.de
www.schmitts-kinder.de

HESSISCHE BERGSTRASSE

Hessische Staatsweingüter Domaine Bergstrasse
Ⓢ
Grieselstrasse 34–36
D-64625 Bensheim
Telephone +49 6251 3107
bergstrasse@
staatsweingueterhessen.de
www.staatsweingueterhessen.de

MITTELRHEIN

Didinger
Ⓑ Ⓓ Ⓢ
Rheinuferstrasse 13
D-56340 Osterspai
Telephone +49 2627 512
weingutdidinger@web.de
www.weingut-didinger.de

Toni Jost – Hahnenhof
Ⓑ Ⓓ Ⓕ Ⓢ
Oberstrasse 14
D-55422 Bacharach
Telephone +49 6743 1216
tonijost@debitel.net

Matthias Müller
Ⓑ Ⓓ Ⓕ Ⓢ
Mainzer Strasse 45
D-56322 Spay am Rhein
Telephone +49 2628 8741
weingut.matthias.mueller
@t-online.de
(see page 104)

Ratzenberger
Ⓑ Ⓓ Ⓕ Ⓢ
Blücherstrasse 167
D-55422 Bacharach
Telephone +49 6743 1337
weingut-ratzenberger@t-online.de
www.weingut-ratzenberger.de

Florian Weingart
Ⓑ Ⓓ Ⓢ
Mainzer Strasse 32
D-56322 Spay am Rhein
Telephone +49 2628 8735
info@weingut-weingart.de
www.weingart-wein.de
(see page 114)

MOSEL-SAAR-RUWER

Clemens Busch
Ⓓ Ⓕ Ⓜ Ⓢ
Kirchstrasse 37
D-56862 Pünderich
Telephone +49 6542 22180
weingut@clemens-busch.de
www.clemens-busch.de
(see page 106)

Ansgar Clüsserath
Ⓑ Ⓓ Ⓕ Ⓢ
Spielestrasse 4
D-54349 Trittenheim
Telephone +49 6507 2290
weingut@ansgar-cluesserath.de
www.ansgar-cluesserath.de
(see page 113)

Ⓑ A sound basis   Ⓓ Fruity diversity   Ⓔ Complex elegance   Ⓕ Delicate finesse   Ⓜ Baroque monuments   Ⓢ Noble sweetness

Clüsserath-Weiler
B **F** **S**

Haus an der Brücke
D-54349 Trittenheim
Telephone +49 6507 5011
helmut@cluesserath-weiler.de
www.cluesserath-weiler.de

Grans-Fassian
D **F** **S**

Römerstrasse 28
D-54340 Leiwen
Telephone +49 6507 3170
weingut@grans-fassian.de
www.grans-fassian.de

Fritz Haag
D **F** **S**

Dusemonder Hof
D-54472 Braneberg
Telephone +49 6534 410
weingut-fritz-haag@t-online.de
www.weingut-fritz-haag.de
(see page 116)

Reinhold Haart
D **F** **S**

Ausoniusufer 18
D-54498 Piesport
Telephone +49 6507 2015
info@haart.de
www.haart.de
(see page 105)

Heymann-Löwenstein
M **S**

Bahnhofstrasse 10
D-56333 Winningen
Telephone +49 2606 1919
reinhard@heymann-
loewenstein.com
www.heymann-loewenstein.com

Von Hövel
D **F** **S**

Agritiusstrasse 5–6
D-54329 Konz-Oberemmel
Telephone +49 6501 15384
weingutvonhoevel@t-online.de

Karlsmühle
B **F** **S**

Im Ruwertal
D-54318 Mertesdorf-Lorenzhof
Telephone +49 651 5124
anfrage@weingut-karlsmuehle.de
www.weingut-karlsmuehle.de

Karthäuserhof
D **F** **S**

D-54292 Trier-Eitelsbach
Telephone +49 651 5121
mail@karthaeuserhof.com
www.karthaeuserhof.com

Reichsgraf von Kesselstatt
D **F** **S**

Schlossgut Marienlay
D-54317 Morscheid
Telephone +49 6500 916 90
weingut@kesselstatt.com
www.kesselstatt.com
(see page 106)

Kirsten
B **D** **S**

Krainstrasse 5
D-54340 Klüsserath
Telephone +49 6507 99115
mail@weingut-kirsten.de
www.weingut-kirsten.de

Reinhard und Beate Knebel
D **S**

August-Horch-Strasse 24
D-56333 Winningen
Telephone +49 2606 2631
info@weingut-knebel.de

Schloss Lieser
D **F** **S**

Am Markt 1–5
D-54470 Lieser
Telephone +49 6531 6431
info@weingut-schloss-lieser.de
www.weingut-schloss-lieser.de
(see page 116)

Dr. Loosen
D **F** **S**

St. Johannishof
D-54470 Bernkastel-Kues
Telephone +49 6531 3426
vertrieb@drloosen.de
www.drloosen.de
(see page 143)

Lubentiushof – Andreas Barth

Kehrstrasse 16
D-56332 Niederfell
Telephone +49 2607 8135
weingut@lubentiushof.de
www.lubentiushof.de

Melsheimer

Dorfstrasse 21
D-56861 Reil
Telephone +49 6542 2422
Thorsten.Melsheimer@t-online.de
www.melsheimer-riesling.de

Markus Molitor
D **S**

Haus Klosterberg
D-54470 Bernkastel-Wehlen
Telephone +49 6532 3939
info@markusmolitor.com
www.markusmolitor.com

Egon Müller – Scharzhof
D **S**

Scharzhof
D-54459 Wiltingen
Telephone +49 6501 17232
egon@scharzhof.de
www.scharzhof.de
(see page 143)

Von Othegraven
D **S**

Weinstrasse 1
D-54441 Kanzem
Telephone +49 6501 150042
von-othegraven@t-online.de
www.von-othegraven.de

B A sound basis   **D** Fruity diversity   **E** Complex elegance   **F** Delicate finesse   **M** Baroque monuments   **S** Noble sweetness

Joh. Jos. Prüm
D F S
Uferallee 19
D-54470 Bernkastel-Wehlen
Telephone +49 6531 3091
(see page 112)

S. A. Prüm
D S
Uferallee 25–26
D-54470 Bernkastel-Wehlen
Telephone +49 6531 3110
info@sapruem.com
www.sapruem.com

St. Urbans-Hof
D F S
Urbanusstrasse 16
D-54340 Leiwen
Telephone +49 6507 93770
st.urbans-hof@t-online.de
www.urbans-hof.de
(see page 114)

Willi Schaefer
D S
Hauptstrasse 130
D-54470 Bernkastel-Graach
Telephone +49 6531 8041

Schloss Saarstein
D F S
Schloss Saarstein
D-54455 Serrig an der Saar
Telephone +49 6581 2324
info@saarstein.de
www.saarstein.de

C. von Schubert'sche Schlosskellerei
D S
Grünhaus bei Trier
D-54318 Mertesdorf
Telephone +49 651 5111
info@vonSchubert.com
www.vonSchubert.com

Heinz Schmitt
B S
Stephanusstrasse 4
D-54340 Leiwen
Telephone +49 6507 4276
info@weingut-heinz-schmitt.de
www.weingut-heinz-schmitt.de

Selbach-Oster
D F S
Uferallee 23
D-54492 Zeltingen-Rachtig
Telephone +49 6532 2081
info@selbach-oster.de
www.selbach-oster.de

Van Volxem
M
Dehenstrasse 2
D-54459 Wiltingen
Telephone +49 6501 16510
vanvolxem@t-online.de
www.vanvolxem.de

Vollenweider
D F S
Wolfer Weg 53
D-56841 Traben-Trarbach
Telephone +49 6541 814433
mail@weingut-vollenweider.de
www.weingut-vollenweider.de

Zimmermann-Graeff & Müller
B
Marientaler Au 23
D-56856 Zell / Mosel
Telephone +49 6542 4190
info@zgm.de
www.zgm.de

NAHE

Dr. Crusius
B D F S
Hauptstrasse 2
D-55595 Traisen
Telephone +49 671 33953
weingut-crusius@t-online.de
www.weingut-crusius.de

Schlossgut Diel
D E F S
D-55452 Burg Layen
Telephone +49 6721 96950
info@schlossgut-diel.com
www.schlossgut-diel.com

Hermann Dönnhoff
D E F S
Bahnhofstrasse 11
D-55585 Oberhausen
Telephone +49 6755 263
weingut@doennhoff.com
www.doennhoff.de
(see page 146)

Emrich-Schönleber
D E F S
Naheweinstrasse 10 a
D-55569 Monzingen
Telephone +49 6751 2733
weingut@emrich-schoenleber.com
www.emrich-schoenleber.com
(see page 124)

Hexamer
B D S
Sobernheimer Strasse 3
D-55566 Meddersheim
Telephone +49 6751 2269
Weingut-hexamer@t-online.de
www.weingut-hexamer.de

B A sound basis **D** Fruity diversity **E** Complex elegance **F** Delicate finesse **M** Baroque monuments **S** Noble sweetness

Korrell – Johanneshof
Ⓑ Ⓓ
Parkstrasse 4
D-55545 Bad Kreuznach
Telephone +49 671 63630
Weingut-korrell@t-online.de
www.weingut-korrell.de

Reh-Kendermann GmbH
Weinkellerei
Ⓑ
Am Ockenheimer Graben 35
D- 55411 Bingen-Rhein
Telephone +49 6721 9010
info@reh-kendermann.de
www.reh-kendermann.de
(see page 100)
Direct purchase is not possible.

Kruger-Rumpf
Ⓑ Ⓓ Ⓕ
Rheinstrasse 47
D-55424 Münster-Sarmsheim
Telephone +49 6721 43859
info@kruger-rumpf.com
www.kruger-rumpf.com

Gutsverwaltung Niederhausen-
Schlossböckelheim
Ehemalige Weinbaudomäne
D-55585 Niederhausen
Telephone +49 6758 92500
info@riesling-domaene.de
www.riesling-domaene.de

Prinz zu Salm-Dalberg'sches
Weingut
Schloss Wallhausen
Schlossstrasse 3
D-55595 Wallhausen
Telephone +49 6706 94440
Salm.dalberg@salm-salm.de
www.salm-salm.de

Joh. Babt. Schäfer
Ⓑ Ⓓ Ⓢ
Burg Layen 8
D-55452 Burg Layen
Telephone +49 6721 43552
schaefer@jbs-wein.de
www.jbs-wein.de
(see page 98)

Schäfer-Fröhlich
Ⓓ Ⓔ Ⓢ
Schulstrasse 6
D-55595 Bockenau
Telephone +49 6758 6521
info@weingut-schaefer-froehlich.de
www.weingut-schaefer-froehlich.de

Bürgermeister Schweinhardt
Ⓑ Ⓢ
Heddesheimer Strasse 1
D-55450 Langenlonsheim
Telephone +49 6704 93100
info@schweinhardt.de
www.schweinhardt.de

Tesch
Naheweinstrasse 99
D-55450 Langenlonsheim
Telephone +49 6704 93040
info@weingut-tesch.de
www.weingut-tesch.de

WIV Wein International AG
Ⓑ
Hauptstrasse 1
D-55452 Burg Layen
Telephone +49 6721 9650
info@wiv-ag.com
www.wiv-ag.com

P F A L Z

Acham-Magin
Weinstrasse 67
D-67147 Forst an der Weinstrasse
Telephone +49 6326 315
info@acham-magin.de
www.acham-magin.de

Geheimer Rat
Dr. von Bassermann-Jordan
Ⓓ Ⓔ Ⓢ
Kirchgasse 10
D-67142 Deidesheim
Telephone +49 6326 6006
hauck@bassermann-jordan.de
www.bassermann-jordan.de
(see page 148)

Bergdolt – Sankt Lamprecht
Ⓑ Ⓢ
Dudostrasse 17
D-67435 Neustadt-Duttweiler
Telephone +49 6327 5027
weingut-bergdolt-st.lamprecht
@t-online.de
www.weingut-bergdolt.de

Dr. Bürklin-Wolf'sche
Gutsverwaltung GmbH
Ⓜ Ⓢ
Weinstrasse 65
D-67157 Wachenheim
Telephone +49 6322 95330
bb@buerklin-wolf.de
www.buerklin-wolf.de

A. Christmann
Ⓑ Ⓜ Ⓢ
Peter-Koch-Strasse 43
D-67435 Gimmeldingen
Telephone +49 6321 66039
weingut.christmann@t-online.de
www.weingut-christmann.de
(see page 132)

Gies-Düppel
Am Rosenberg 5
D-76831 Birkweiler
Telephone +49 6345 919156
weingutgies@aol.com

Ⓑ A sound basis   Ⓓ Fruity diversity   Ⓔ Complex elegance   Ⓕ Delicate finesse   Ⓜ Baroque monuments   Ⓢ Noble sweetness

Thomas Hensel
Ⓑ
In den Almen 13
D-67098 Bad Dürkheim
Telephone +49 6322 2460
henselwein@aol.com
www.weingut-hensel.de

Knipser Johannishof
Ⓜ
Hauptstrasse 47
D-67229 Laumersheim
Telephone +49 6238 742
mail@weingut-knipser.de
www.weingut-knipser.de

Koehler-Ruprecht
Ⓜ
Weinstrasse 84
D-67169 Kallstadt
Telephone +49 6322 1829
berndphilippi@t-online.de
(see page 134)

Kranz
Ⓑ
Mörzheimer Strasse 2
D-76831 Ilbesheim
Telephone +49 6341 939206
weingut-kranz@t-online.de
www.weingut-kranz.de
(see page 97)

Philipp Kuhn
Grosskarlbacher Strasse 20
D-67229 Laumersheim
Telephone +49 6238 656
weingut-philipp-kuhn@gmx.de

Georg Mosbacher
Ⓑ Ⓔ Ⓢ
Weinstrasse 27
D-67147 Forst
Telephone +49 6326 329
mosbacher@t-online.de
www.georg-mosbacher.de

Müller-Catoir
Ⓓ Ⓢ
Haardt an der Weinstrasse
Mandelring 25
D-67433 Neustadt an der
Weinstrasse
Telephone +49 6321 2815
weingut@mueller-catoir.de
www.mueller-catoir.de

Ludi Neiss
Ⓑ
Hauptstrasse 91
D-67271 Kindenheim
Telephone +49 6359 4327
weingut-neiss@t-online.de

Karl Pfaffmann
Ⓑ Ⓢ
Allmendstrasse 1
D-76833 Walsheim
Telephone +49 6341 61856
info@weingut-karl-pfaffmann.de
www.weingut-karl-pfaffmann.de

Rolf Pfaffmann
Am Stahlbühl
D-76833 Frankweiler
Telephone +49 6345 1364
R-T-Pfaffmann@t-online.de
www.wein-pfaffmann.de

Pfeffingen
Fuhrmann-Eymael
Deutsche Weinstrasse
D-67098 Bad Dürkheim
Telephone +49 6322 8607
pfeffingen@t-online.de
www.pfeffingen.de

Ökonomierat Rebholz
Ⓔ Ⓕ Ⓢ
Weinstrasse 54
D-76833 Siebeldingen
Telephone +49 6345 3439
wein@oekonomierat-rebholz.de
www.oekonomierat-rebholz.de
(see page 123)

Egon Schmitt
Am Neuberg 6
D-67098 Bad Dürkheim
Telephone +49 6322 5830
info@weingut-egon-schmitt.de
www.weingut-egon-schmitt.de

Klaus Schneider
Georg-Fitz-Strasse 12
D-67158 Ellerstadt
Telephone +49 6237 7288
weingut-schneider@t-online.de

Ullrichshof
Familie Faubel
Marktstrasse 86
D-67487 Maikammer
Telephone +49 6321 5048
info@ullrichshof-faubel.de
www.ullrichshof-faubel.de

Weegmüller
Mandelring 23
D-67433 Neustadt-Haardt
Telephone +49 6321 83772
info@weegmueller.de
www.weegmueller-weine.de

Dr. Wehrheim
Ⓜ Ⓢ
Weinstrasse 8
D-76831 Birkweiler
Telephone +49 6345 3542
dr.wehrheim@t-online.de
www.weingut-wehrheim.de

RHEINGAU

Fritz Allendorf
Ⓑ Ⓓ
Kirchstrasse 69
D-65375 Oestrich-Winkel
Telephone +49 6723 91850
allendorf@allendorf.de
www.allendorf.de

Ⓑ A sound basis   **Ⓓ** Fruity diversity   **Ⓔ** Complex elegance   **Ⓕ** Delicate finesse   **Ⓜ** Baroque monuments   **Ⓢ** Noble sweetness

Friedrich Altenkirch

Ⓑ Ⓕ

Binger Weg 2
D-65391 Lorch
Telephone +49 6726 830012
info@weingut-altenkirch.de
www.weingut-altenkirch.de
(see page 104)

J. B. Becker

Ⓜ Ⓢ

Rheinstrasse 6
D-65396 Walluf
Telephone +49 6123 72523
h.j.becker@justmail.de
(see page 134)

Georg Breuer

Ⓔ Ⓢ

Grabenstrasse 8
D-65385 Rüdesheim am Rhein
Telephone +49 6722 1027
info@georg-breuer.com
www.georg-breuer.com
(see page 125)

Joachim Flick
Weingut in der Strassenmühle

Ⓑ Ⓕ Ⓢ

Strassenmühle
D-65439 Flörsheim-Wicker
Telephone +49 6145 7686
info@flick-wein.de
www.flick-wein.de
(see page 109)

Johannishof
Familie Eser

Grund 63
D-65366 Johannisberg
Telephone +49 6722 8216
info@weingut-johannishof.de
www.weingut-johannishof.de

Schloss Johannisberg

Ⓢ

Schloss Johannisberger
Weingüterverwaltung
D-65366 Geisenheim-Johannisberg
Telephone +49 6722 70090
info@schloss-johannisberg.de
www.schloss-johannisberg.de

Jakob Jung

Eberbacher Strasse 22
D-65346 Erbach
Telephone +49 6123 900620
info@weingut-jakob-jung.de
www.weingut-jakob-jung.de

August Kesseler

Ⓢ

Lorcher Strasse 16
D-65385 Assmannshausen
Telephone +49 6722 2513
info@august-kesseler.de
www.august-kesseler.de

Klosterweingut
Abtei St. Hildegard

Ⓑ

Klosterweg 1
D-65385 Rüdesheim am Rhein
Telephone +49 6722 499130
weingut@abtei-st-hildegard.de
www.abtei-st-hildegard.de
(see page 101)

Peter Jakob Kühn

Ⓑ Ⓢ

Mühlstrasse 70
D-65375 Oestrich
Telephone +49 6723 2299
info@weingutpjkuehn.de
www.weingutpjkuehn.de

Franz Künstler

Ⓜ Ⓢ

Kirchstrasse 38
D-65239 Hochheim am Main
Telephone +49 6146 83860
info@weingut-kuenstler.de
www.weingut-kuenstler.de,
(see page 133)

Hans Lang

Rheinallee 6
D-65347 Eltville-Hattenheim
Telephone +49 6723 2475
langwein@t-online.de
www.weingut-hans-lang.de

Langwerth von Simmern

Ⓓ Ⓢ

Kirchgasse 6
D-65343 Eltville
Telephone +49 6123 92110
weingut@langwerth-von-
simmern.de
www.langwerth-von-simmern.de

Josef Leitz

Ⓓ Ⓜ Ⓢ

Theodor-Heuss-Strasse 5
D-65385 Rüdesheim am Rhein
Telephone +49 6722 48711
info@leitz-wein.de
www.leitz-wein.de

Fürst Löwenstein

Ⓑ Ⓢ

Niederwaldstrasse 8
D-65375 Oestrich-Winkel /
Hallgarten
Telephone +49 6723 999770
hallgarten@loewenstein.de
www.loewenstein.de

Prinz

Ⓑ Ⓢ

Im Flachsgarten 5
D-65375 Hallgarten
Telephone +49 6723 999847
prinzfred@gmx.de

Schloss Reinhartshausen

Ⓢ

Hauptstrasse 41
D-65346 Eltville-Erbach
Telephone +49 6123 676333
service@schloss-reinhartshausen.de
www.schloss-reinhartshausen.de

Ⓑ A sound basis   Ⓓ Fruity diversity   Ⓔ Complex elegance   Ⓕ Delicate finesse   Ⓜ Baroque monuments   Ⓢ Noble sweetness

Domänenweingut
Schloss Schönborn
Hauptstrasse 53
D-65347 Eltville-Hattenheim
Telephone +49 6723 91810
schloss-schoenborn
@schoenborn.de
www.schoenborn.de

Schloss Vollrads
Ⓓ Ⓕ Ⓢ
D-65375 Oestrich-Winkel
Telephone +49 6723 660
info@schlossvollrads.com
www.schlossvollrads.com
(see page 107)

Josef Spreitzer
Ⓓ Ⓜ Ⓢ
Rheingaustrasse 86
D-65375 Oestrich
Telephone +49 6723 2625
weingut-spreitzer@t-online.de
www.weingut-spreitzer.de
(see page 117)

Hessische Staatsweingüter GmbH
Kloster Eberbach
Schwalbacher Strasse 56–62
D-65343 Eltville am Rhein
Telephone +49 6123 92300
info@weingut-kloster-eberbach.de
www.weingut-kloster-eberbach.de

Geheimrat J. Wegeler Erben
Friedensplatz 9–11
D-65375 Oestrich-Winkel
Telephone +49 6723 99090
info@wegeler.com
www.wegeler.com

Robert Weil
Ⓓ Ⓔ Ⓕ Ⓢ
Mühlberg 5
D-65399 Kiedrich
Telephone +49 6123 2308
info@weingut-robert-weil.com
www.weingut-robert-weil.com
(see page 144)

RHEINHESSEN

Battenfeld Spanier
Ⓑ Ⓢ
Bahnhofstrasse 33
D-67591 Hohen-Sülzen
Telephone +49 6243 906515
kontakt@battenfeld-spanier.de
www.battenfeld-spanier.de

Brüder Dr. Becker
Familie Pfeffer-Müller
Mainzer Strasse 3–7
D-55278 Ludwigshöhe
Telephone +49 6249 8430
lotte.pfeffer@brueder-dr-becker.de
www.brueder-dr-becker.de

Frieder Dreissigacker
Ⓑ
Untere Klinggasse 4
D-67595 Bechtheim
Telephone +49 6242 2425
info@dreissigacker-wein.de
www.dreissigacker-wein.de
(see page 99)

Fogt
Ⓑ
Schönborner Hof
D-55576 Badenheim
Telephone +49 6701 7434
WeingutFogt@t-online.de
www.weingut-fogt.de

Gehring
Ⓑ Ⓓ
Ausserhalb 17
D-55283 Nierstein
Telephone +49 6133 5470
info@weingut-gehring.com
www.weingut-gehring.com

Ökonomierat Joh. Geil I. Erben
Ⓑ Ⓢ
Kuhpfortenstrasse 11
D-67595 Bechtheim
Telephone +49 6242 1546
kontakt@weingut-geil.de
www.weingut-geil.de

K. F. Groebe
Ⓓ Ⓢ
Bahnhofstrasse 68–70
D-64584 Biebesheim
Telephone +49 6258 6721
weingut.k.f.groebe@t-online.de
www.weingut-k-f-groebe.de

Gunderloch
Ⓓ Ⓕ Ⓢ
Carl-Gunderloch-Platz 1
D-55299 Nackenheim
Telephone +49 6135 2341
info@gunderloch.de
www.gunderloch.de

Gutzler
Ⓑ Ⓢ
Rossgasse 19
D-67599 Gundheim
Telephone +49 6244 905221
info@gutzler.de
www.gutzler.de

Freiherr Heyl zu Herrnsheim
Langgasse 3
D-55283 Nierstein
Telephone +49 6133 57080
info@heyl-zu-herrnsheim.de
www.heyl-zu-herrnsheim.de

Keller
Ⓔ Ⓢ
Bahnhofstrasse 1
D-67592 Flörsheim-Dalsheim
Telephone +49 6243 456
info@keller-wein.de
www.weingut-keller.de
(see page 145)

Kühling-Gillot
Ölmühlstrasse 25
D-55294 Bodenheim
Telephone +49 6135 2333
info@kuehling-gillot.de
www.kuehling-gillot.de

Ⓑ A sound basis   Ⓓ Fruity diversity   Ⓔ Complex elegance   Ⓕ Delicate finesse   Ⓜ Baroque monuments   Ⓢ Noble sweetness

Manz
Ⓑ
Lettengasse 6
D-55278 Weinolsheim
Telephone +49 6249 7981
weingut@manz-weinolsheim.de
www.manz-weinolsheim.de

Michel-Pfannebecker
Ⓑ
Langgasse 18/19
D-55234 Flomborn
Telephone +49 6735 1363
wgtmi.pfa@t-online.de
www.michel-pfannebecker.de

St. Antony
Wörrstädter Strasse 22
D-55283 Nierstein
Telephone +49 6133 5482
st.antony@t-online.de
www.st-antony.com

Scherner-Kleinhanss
Ⓑ
Alzeyer Strasse 10
D-67592 Flörsheim-Dalsheim
Telephone +49 6243 435
info@scherner-kleinhanss.de
www.scherner-kleinhanss.de
(see page 97)

Georg Albrecht Schneider
Ⓑ
Wilhelmstrasse 6
D-55283 Nierstein
Telephone +49 6133 5655
info@schneider-nierstein.de
www.schneider-nierstein.de

P. J. Valckenberg
Ⓑ
Postfach 2345
D-67513 Worms
Telephone +49 6274 91110
info@valckenberg.com
www.valckenberg.com

Wagner-Stempel
Ⓑ Ⓔ
Wöllsteinerstrasse 10
D-55599 Siefersheim
Telephone +49 6703 960330
info@wagner-stempel.de
www.wagner-stempel.de

Winter
Ⓑ
Hauptstrasse 17
D-67596 Dittelsheim-Hessloch
Telephone +49 6244 7446
info@weingut-winter.de
www.weingut-winter.de

Wittmann
Ⓑ Ⓢ
Mainzer Strasse 19
D-67593 Westhofen bei Worms
Telephone +49 6244 905036
info@wittmannweingut.com
www.wittmannweingut.com
(see page 122)

SAALE-UNSTRUT

Bernard Pawis
Lauchaer Strasse 31c
D-06632 Freyburg
Telephone +49 34464 28315
info@weingut-pawis.de
www.weingut-pawis.de

SAXONY

Schloss Proschwitz
Prinz zur Lippe
Dorfanger 19
D-01665 Zadel über Meissen
Telephone +49 3521 76760
schloss-proschwitz@t-online.de
www.schloss-proschwitz.de

Zimmerling
Bergweg 27
D-01326 Dresden-Pillnitz
Telephone +49 351 2618752

WÜRTTEMBERG

Graf Adelmann
Auf Burg Schaubeck
D-71711 Steinheim-Kleinbottwar
Telephone +49 7148 921220
weingut@graf-adelmann.com
www.graf-adelmann.com

Gerhard Aldinger
Ⓑ Ⓢ
Schmerstrasse 25
D-70734 Fellbach
Telephone +49 711 581417
info@weingut-aldinger.de
www.weingut-aldinger.de

Beurer
Lange Strasse 67
D-71394 Kernen-Stetten i. R.
Telephone +49 7151 42190
info@weingut-beurer.de
www.weingut-beurer.de

Ernst Dautel
Ⓑ Ⓢ
Lauerweg 55
D-74357 Bönnigheim
Telephone +49 7143 870326
info@weingut-dautel.de
www.weingut-dautel.de

Karl Haidle
Hindenburgstrasse 21
D-71394 Kernen-Stetten
Telephone +49 7151 949110
info@weingut-karl-haidle.de
www.weingut-karl-haidle.de

Fürst zu Hohenlohe-Oehringen
Im Schloss
D-74613 Öhringen
Telephone +49 7941 94910
info@verrenberg.de
www.verrenberg.de

Ⓑ A sound basis   Ⓓ Fruity diversity   Ⓔ Complex elegance   Ⓕ Delicate finesse   Ⓜ Baroque monuments   Ⓢ Noble sweetness

Rainer Schnaitmann
Untertürkheimer Strasse 4
D-70734 Fellbach
Telephone +49 711 574616
weingut.schnaitmann@t-online.de
www.weingut-schnaitmann.de

Hans-Peter Wöhrwag
Grunbacherstrasse 5
D-70327 Stuttgart-Untertürkheim
Telephone +49 711 331662
info@woehrwag.de
www.woehrwag.de

FRANCE

ALSACE

Domaine Bernhard-Reibel
20, rue de Lorraine
F-67730 Châtenois
Telephone +33 388 820421
bernhard-reibel@wanadoo.fr

Léon Beyer
2, rue de la première armée
F-68420 Eguisheim
Telephone +33 389 216230
contact@leonbeyer.fr
www.leonbeyer.fr

Domaine Paul Blanck
E
32, Grande-Rue / BP 55
F-68240 Kientzheim
Telephone +33 389 782356
info@blanck.com
www.blanck-alsace.com

Domaine Marcel Deiss
M
15, Route du Vin
F-68750 Bergheim
Telephone +33 389 736337
marceldeiss@marceldeiss.com
www.marceldeiss.com

Paul Ginglinger
8, place Charles-de-Gaulle
F-68420 Eguisheim
Telephone +33 389 414425
info@paul-ginglinger.fr
www.paul-ginglinger.fr

Domaine André & Rémy Gresser
M S
2, rue de l'école
F-67140 Andlau
Telephone +33 388 089588
remy.gresser@wanadoo.fr

Domaine Pierre Hering
S
6, rue Sultzer
F-67140 Barr
Telephone +33 388 089007
jdh@infonie.fr
www.vins-hering.com

Hugel et Fils
M S
3, rue de la première armée
F-68640 Riquewihr
Telephone +33 389 479215
info@hugel.com
www.hugel.com

Josmeyer & Fils S.A.
76, rue Clémenceau
F-68920 Wintzenheim
Telephone +33 389 279190
contact@josmeyer.com
www.josmeyer.com

Domaine André Kientzler
E S
50, route de Bergheim
F-68150 Ribeauvillé
Telephone +33 389 736710

Domaine Marc Kreydenweiss
M
12, rue Deharbe
F-67140 Andlau
Telephone +33 388 089583
marc@kreydenweiss.com
www.kreydenweiss.com

Domaine Albert Mann
13, rue du Château
F-68920 Wettolsheim
Telephone +33 389 806200
vins@mann-albert.com

Frédéric Mochel
B
56, rue Principale
F-67310 Traenheim
Telephone +33 388 503867
infos@mochel.net
www.mochel.net

Domaine Ostertag
87, rue Finkwiller
F-67680 Epfig
Telephone +33 388 855134
domaine.ostertag@wanadoo.fr

Cave Vinicole de Ribeauvillé
B
2, route de Colmar
F-68150 Ribeauvillé
Telephone +33 389 736180
cave@cave-ribeauville.com
www.cave-ribeauville.com
(see page 99)

Domaine du Clos Saint Landelin
M S
Route du Vin
F-68250 Rouffach
Telephone +33 389 785800
rene@mure.com
www.mure.com

Domaine Martin Schaetzel
3, rue de la 5e-Division-Blindée
F-68770 Ammerschwihr
Telephone +33 389 471139

Domaine Sylvie Spielmann
S
2, route de Thannenkirch
F-68750 Bergheim
Telephone +33 389 733595
sylvie@sylviespielmann.com
www.sylviespielmann.com

B A sound basis   **D** Fruity diversity   **E** Complex elegance   **F** Delicate finesse   **M** Baroque monuments   **S** Noble sweetness

Trimbach
E S
15, route de Bergheim
F-68150 Ribeauvillé
Telephone +33 389 736030
contact@maison-trimbach.fr
www.maison-trimbach.fr
(see page 129)

Domaine Weinbach
M S
25, Route du Vin
F-68240 Kaysersberg
Telephone +33 389 471321
contact@domaineweinbach.com
www.domaineweinbach.com
(see page 138)

Domaine Zind-Humbrecht
M S
4, Route de Colmar
F-68230 Turckheim
Telephone +33 389 270205
o.humbrecht@wanadoo.fr
(see page 149)

ITALY

SOUTH TYROL

Eisacktaler Kellerei
Leitach 50
I-39043 Klausen
Telephone +39 0472 847553
info@eisacktalerkellerei.it
www.eisacktalerkellerei.it

Köferhof
Günther Kerschbaumer
Via Pusteria 3
I-39040 Novacella / Varna
Telephone +39 0472 836649

Kellerei St. Michael Eppan
Umfahrungsstrasse 17–19
I-39057 Eppan
Telephone +39 0471 664466
kellerei@stmichael.it
www.stmichael.it

LUXEMBOURG

Domaine Viticole Decker Charles
7, route de Mondorf
L-5441 Remerschen
Telephone +352 23 609510
deckerch@pt.lu

Madame Aly Duhr et Fils
9, rue Aly Duhr
L-5401 Ahn
Telephone +352 76 0043
aduhr@pt.lu

Domaine Viticole Alice Hartman
72-74, rue Principale
L-5480 Wormeldange
Telephone +352 76 0002
domainealicehartmann@email.lu

Domaine Viticole Bastian Mathis
29, route de Luxembourg
L-5551 Remich
Telephone +352 23 698295

Château Pauqué
M
73, route de Trèves
L-6793 Grevenmacher
Telephone +352 021 196037
abiduhr@internet.lu

Clos de Rocher
B S
Caves Bernard-Massard
8, rue du Pont
L-6773 Grevenmacher
Telephone +352 75 05451
info@bernard-massard.lu
www.bernard-massard.lu

Caves Sunnen-Hoffmann
B
6, rue des Prés
L-5441 Remerschen
Telephone +352 23 664007
info@caves-sunnen.lu
www.caves-sunnen.lu

AUSTRIA

KAMPTAL

Bründlmayer
M
Zwettlerstrasse 23
A-3550 Langenlois
Telephone +43 2734 21720
weingut@bruendlmayer.at
www.bruendlmayer.at
(see page 137)

Birgit Eichinger
Langenloiserstrasse 365
A-3491 Strass im Strassertal
Telephone +43 2735 56480
office@weingut-eichinger.at
www.weingut-eichinger.at

Schloss Gobelsburg
M
Schlossstrasse 16
A-3550 Langenlois
Telephone +43 2734 2422
schloss@gobelsburg.at
www.gobelsburg.at

B A sound basis   **D** Fruity diversity   **E** Complex elegance   **F** Delicate finesse   **M** Baroque monuments   **S** Noble sweetness

Jurtschitsch Sonnhof
B E
Rudolfstrasse 39
A-3550 Langenlois
Telephone +43 2734 2116
office@jurtschitsch.com
www.jurtschitsch.com

Fred Loimer
E
Kamptalstrasse
A-3550 Langenlois
Telephone +43 2734 2239
weingut@loimer.at
www.loimer.at

KREMSTAL

Martin Nigl
E
Kirchenberg 1
A-3541 Senftenberg
Telephone +43 2719 2609
reservierung@weingutnigl.at
www.weingutnigl.at
(see page 128)

Bertold und Erich
Salomon – Undhof
Undstrasse 10
A-3504 Krems-Stein an der Donau
Telephone +43 2732 83226
salomon@undhof.at
www.undhof.at

WACHAU

Johann Donabaum
Laaben 15
A-3620 Spitz an der Donau
Telephone +43 2713 2488
info@weingut-donabaum.at
www.weingut-donabaum.at

Freie Weingärtner Wachau
B
A-3601 Dürnstein
Telephone +43 2711 371
office@fww.at
www.fww.at

Franz Hirtzberger
M
Kremser Strasse 8
A-3620 Spitz an der Donau
Telephone +43 2713 2209
weingut@hirtzberger.com
www.hirtzberger.com
(see page 136)

Josef Jamek
M
Joching 45
A-3610 Weissenkirchen
Telephone +43 2715 2235
info@weingut-jamek.at
www.jamek.cc

Emmerich Knoll
M S
Unterloiben 10
A-3601 Loiben
Telephone +43 2732 79355
weingut@knoll.at
www.knoll.at
(see page 138)

Franz Xaver Pichler
M
Oberloiben 27
A-3601 Loiben
Telephone +43 2732 85375
winery@fx-pichler.at
www.fx-pichler.at
(see page 136)

Rudolf Pichler
B E
Wösendorf 38
A-3610 Weissenkirchen
Telephone +43 2715 22674
weingut@rudipichler.at

Prager
E
Wachaustrasse 48
A-3610 Weissenkirchen
Telephone +43 2715 2248
prager@weissenkirchen.at
www.weingutprager.at
(see page 126)

Schmelz
F
Weinbergstrasse 14
A-3610 Joching-Weissenkirchen
Telephone +43 2715 2435
info@schmelzweine.at
www.schmelzweine.at
(see page 108)

SPAIN

Miguel Torres, SA
M. Torres, 6
E-08720 Vilafranca del Penedès
Telephone +34 93 8177400
webmaster@torres.es
www.torres.es

PORTUGAL

Niepoort Vinhos S.A.
Rua Infante Dom Henriquez 16-2
P-4050-296 Porto
Telephone information withheld
by request of D. Niepoort.
dirk@niepoort-sa.pt

B A sound basis   **D** Fruity diversity   **E** Complex elegance   **F** Delicate finesse   **M** Baroque monuments   **S** Noble sweetness

SWITZERLAND

Daniel und Martha Gantenbein
D
Platz 34
CH-7306 Fläsch
Telephone +41 81 3024788
(see page 118)

Domaine du Mont d'Or
Pont-de-la-Morge / Sion
Case Postale 240
CH-1964 Conthey 1
Telephone +41 27 3462032
montor@montdor-wine.ch
www.montdor-wine.ch

AUSTRALIA

SOUTH AUSTRALIA

Grosset
E
Stanley Street Auburn
AUS-Auburn, SA 5451
(Clare Valley)
Telephone +61 08 88492175
info@grosset.com.au
www.grosset.com.au
(see page 128)

C. A. Henschke & Co
PO Box 100
AUS-Keyneton, SA 5353
(Eden Valley)
Telephone +61 08 85648223
info@henschke.com.au
www.henschke.com.au

Knappstein Wines
2 Pioneer Avenue
AUS-Clare, SA 5453
(Clare Valley)
Telephone +61 08 88422600
cellardoor@knappsteinwines.
com.au
www.knappsteinwines.com.au

Leasingham
Corporate Headquarters
Hardys Reynella Winery
Reynell Road
AUS-Reynella, SA 5161
(Clare Valley)
Telephone +61 08 83292222
customers@hardys.com.au
www.leasingham-wines.com.au

Mount Horrocks
M
The Old Railway Station
Curling Street
AUS-Auburn, SA 5451
(Clare Valley)
Telephone +61 08 88492243
sales@mounthorrocks.com
www.mounthorrocks.com

Orlando Wyndham
B
Orlando Wyndham Group Pty Ltd
33 Exeter Terrace
AUS-Devon Park, SA 5008
Telephone +61 08 82082444
contact_us@orlando.com.au
www.orlandowyndhamgroup.com

Petaluma
Distinguished Vineyards
Level 11, 20 Hunter Street
AUS-Sydney, NSW 2000
Telephone +61 1300 780785
Riesling-Production:
Petaluma Clare Estate
Spring Gully Road
AUS-Piccadilly, SA 5151
(Clare Valley)
Telephone +61 08 83394122
Petaluma@petaluma.com.au
www.petaluma.com.au

WESTERN AUSTRALIA

Alkoomi
B S
RMB 234
AUS-Frankland, WA 6396
Telephone +61 08 98552229
info@alkoomiwines.com.au
www.alkoomiwines.com.au

Frankland Estate
M
Frankland Road
AUS-Frankland, WA 6396
Telephone +61 08 98551544
info@franklandestate.com.au
www.franklandestate.com.au

Leeuwin Estate Winery
Stevens Road
AUS-Margaret River, WA 6285
Telephone +61 08 97590000
winery@leeuwinestate.com.au
www.leeuwinestate.com.au

TASMANIA

Tamar Ridge Winery
B
Auburn Road
Kayena, Tasmania 7270
Telephone +61 03 63941114
cellardoor@tamarridgewines.
com.au
www.tamarridgewines.com.au

B A sound basis   **D** Fruity diversity   **E** Complex elegance   **F** Delicate finesse   **M** Baroque monuments   **S** Noble sweetness

NEW ZEALAND

NORTH ISLAND

Dry River Wines Limited
PO Box 72
Martinborough
NZ-South Wairarapa
Telephone +64 06 3069388
info@dryriver.co.nz
www.dryriver.co.nz

The Millton Vineyard Ltd
Ⓜ
PO Box 66
NZ-Manutuke, Gisborne
Telephone +64 06 8628680
info@millton.co.nz
www.millton.co.nz

SOUTH ISLAND

CANTERBURY

Giesen Estate
Ⓑ
Burnham School Road
NZ-Burnham, Christchurch
Telephone +64 03 3476729
info@giesen.co.nz
www.giesen.co.nz

Pegasus Bay
Stockgrove Road RD2
NZ-Waipara, North Canterbury
Telephone +64 03 3146869
info@pegasusbay.com
www.pegasusbay.com

CENTRAL OTAGO

Felton Road Wines
Ⓔ Ⓢ
Felton Road
NZ-Bannockburn, Central Otago
Telephone +64 03 4450885
wines@feltonroad.com
www.feltonroad.com

MARLBOROUGH

Allan Scott Wines
Jacksons Road, RD3
NZ-Blenheim, Marlborough
Telephone +64 03 5729054
info@allanscott.com
www.allanscott.com

Framingham Wine Company Ltd
Ⓢ
Conders Bend Road, Marlborough
NZ-Renwich
Telephone +64 03 5728884
info@framingham.co.nz
www.framingham.co.nz

Fromm Winery La Strada
Ⓢ
Godfrey Road, RD2
NZ-Blenheim, Marlborough
Telephone +64 03 5729355
lastrada@frommwineries.com
www.frommwineries.com

Seresin Estate
Bedford Road, PO Box 859
NZ-Blenheim, Marlborough
Telephone +64 03 5729408
info@seresin.co.nz
www.seresin.co.nz

USA

CALIFORNIA

Bonny Doon Vineyard
Ⓑ
2125 Delaware Street Suite E
USA-Santa Cruz, CA 95060
Telephone +1 831 4253625
www.bonnydoonvineyard.com

Freemark Abbey
3022 St. Helena Highway North
USA-St. Helena, CA 94574
Telephone +1 800 9639698
wineinfo@freemarkabbey.com
www.freemarkabbey.com

Château St. Jean
8555 Sonoma Highway
(Highway 12)
PO Box 293
USA-Kenwood, CA 95452
Telephone +1 707 8334134
www.chateaustjean.com

**Smith-Madrone
Vineyards & Winery**
4022 Spring Mountain Road
USA-St. Helena, CA 94574
Telephone +1 707 9632283
info@smithmadrone.com
www.smithmadrone.com

Trefethen
1160 Oak Knoll Avenue
USA-Napa, CA 94558
Telephone +1 707 2557700
winery@trefethen.com
www.trefethen.com

Ⓑ A sound basis   Ⓓ Fruity diversity   Ⓔ Complex elegance   Ⓕ Delicate finesse   Ⓜ Baroque monuments   Ⓢ Noble sweetness

OREGON

Amity Vineyards
18150 Amity Vineyards Road
USA-Amity, OR 97101
Telephone +1 503 8352362
amity@amityvineyards.com
www.amityvineyards.com

Argyle Winery
691 Highway 99W
USA-Dundee, OR 97115
Telephone +1 503 5388520
tastingroom@argylewinery.com
www.argylewinery.com

Elk Cove Vineyards
27751 NW Olson Road
USA-Gaston, OR 97119
Telephone +1 503 9857760
info@elkcove.com
www.elkcove.com

Scott Henry Estate
PO Box 26
USA-Umpqua, OR 97486
Telephone +1 541 4595120
henryest@wizzards.net
www.henryestate.com

NEW YORK STATE

**Dr. Konstantin Frank
Vinifera Wine Cellars**
9749 Middle Road
USA-Hammondsport, NY 14840
Telephone +1 800 3200735
info@drfrankwines.com
www.drfrankwines.com

Hosmer Winery
6999 State Route 89
USA-Ovid, NY 14521
Telephone +1 607 8693393
info@hosmerwinery.com
www.hosmerwinery.com

Lamoreaux Landing Wine Cellars
Ⓑ Ⓢ
9224 Route 414
USA-Lodi, NY 14860-9641
Telephone +1 607 5826011
llwc@capital.net
www.lamoreauxwine.com

Hermann J. Wiemer Vineyard
Ⓓ Ⓕ Ⓢ
PO Box 38
USA-Dundee, NY 14837
Telephone +1 800 3717971
wines@wiemer.com
www.wiemer.com
(see page 119)

WASHINGTON

Badger Mountain Vineyard
Ⓑ
1106 S Jurupa Street
USA-Kennewick, WA 99338-1001
Telephone +1 509 6274986
sales@badgermtnvineyard.com
www.badgermtnvineyard.com

Columbia Winery
Ⓑ
14030 NE 145th Street
PO Box 1248
USA-Woodinville, WA 98072-1248
Telephone +1 425 4882776
contact@columbiawinery.com
www.columbiawinery.com

**Longshadows
Wineries & Vineyards**
P.O. Box 33670
USA-Seattle, WA 98133-0670
Telephone +1 206 3969628
info@longshadows.com
www.longshadows.com

Chateau Ste Michelle
Ⓑ
14111 NE 145th
USA-Woodinville, WA 98072
Telephone +1 425 4881133
info@ste-michelle.com
www.ste-michelle.com

Woodward Canyon Winery
11920 West Highway 12
USA-Lowden, WA 99360
Telephone +1 509 5254129
info@woodwardcanyon.com
www.woodwardcanyon.com

CANADA

BRITISH COLUMBIA

Domaine Combret Estate
32057 #13 Road
CAN-Oliver, BC V0H 1T0
Telephone +1 250 4986966
info@combretwine.com
www.combretwine.com

**Gehringer Brothers
Estate Winery**
Ⓢ
Highway 97, Road 8
CAN-Oliver, BC V0H 1TD
Telephone +1 250 4983537
info@sunnyosoyoos.com
www.sunnyosoyoos.com/webs/
wine/gehringer.htm

Mission Hill
Ⓑ Ⓢ
1730 Mission Hill Road
CAN-Westbank, Okanagan Valley,
BC V4T 2E4
Telephone +1 250 7687611
info@missionhillwinery.com
www.missionhillwinery.com

Ⓑ A sound basis   Ⓓ Fruity diversity   Ⓔ Complex elegance   Ⓕ Delicate finesse   Ⓜ Baroque monuments   Ⓢ Noble sweetness

Quails Gate Estate
3303 Boucherie Road
CAN-Kelowna, BC V1Z 2H3
Telephone +1 250 7694451
info@quailsgate.com
www.quailsgate.com

ONTARIO

Cave Spring Cellars
3836 Main Street
CAN-Jordan, Ontario
Telephone +1 905 5623581
info@cavespring.ca
www.cavespringcellars.com

Inniskillin Wines Inc.
Ⓢ
S.R. #66, RR#1
Niagara Parkway
CAN-Niagara-on-the-Lake,
Ontario L0S 1J0
Telephone +1 905 4682187
inniskil@inniskillin.com
www.inniskillin.com
(see page 149)

**Jackson-Triggs Niagara
Estate Winery**
Ⓢ
2145 Regional Road 55
CAN-Niagara-on-the-Lake,
Ontario L0S 1J0
Telephone +1 905 4684637
niagaraestate
@jacksontriggswinery.com
www.jacksontriggswinery.com

Konzelmann Estate Winery
1096 Lakeshore Road, RR#3
CAN-Niagara-on-the-Lake,
Ontario L0S 1J0
Telephone +1 905 9352866
wine@konzelmannwines.com
www.konzelmannwines.com

Daniel Lenko Estate Winery
5246 Regional Road 81
CAN-Beamsville Ontario L0R 1B3
Telephone +1 905 5637756
oldvines@daniellenko.com
www.daniellenko.com

Thirty Bench Vineyard & Winery
4281 Mountainview Road
CAN-Beamsville, Ontario L0R 1B0
Telephone +1 905 5631698
wine@thirtybench.com
www.thirtybench.com

Vineland Estates Winery
Ⓕ Ⓢ
3620 Moyer Road
CAN-Vineland, Ontario L0R 2C0
Telephone +1 905 5627088
wine@vineland.com
www.vineland.com

SOUTH AFRICA

CONSTANTIA

Buitenverwachting
Klein Constantia Road
P.O. Box 281
RSA-Constantia 7848
Telephone +27 21 7945190
info@buitenverwachting.com
www.buitenverwachting.com

Klein Constantia Estate
P.O. Box 375
RSA-Constantia 7848
Telephone +27 21 7945188
info@kleinconstantia.com
www.kleinconstantia.com

ELGIN

Paul Cluver Wines
P.O. Box 48
RSA-Grabouw 7160
Telephone +27 21 8440605
info@cluver.co.za
www.cluver.co.za

ROBERTSON

De Wetshof Estate
Ⓑ
P.O. Box 31
RSA-Robertson 6705
Telephone +27 23 6151853
info@dewetshof.com
www.dewetshof.com

STELLENBOSCH

Hartenberg Estate
P.O. Box 69
RSA-Koelenhof 7605
Telephone +27 21 8652541
info@hartenbergestate.com
www.hartenbergestate.com

Kathy & Gary Jordan
Ⓑ Ⓢ
Stellenbosch Kloof Rd
RSA-Vlottenburg 7604
Telephone +27 21 8813441
info@jordanwines.com
www.jordanwines.com

Thelema Mountain Vineyards
Helshoogte Pass
P.O. Box 2234
RSA-Stellenbosch 7601
Telephone +27 21 8851924
wines@thelema.co.za
www.thelema.co.za

Ⓑ A sound basis　　Ⓓ Fruity diversity　　Ⓔ Complex elegance　　Ⓕ Delicate finesse　　Ⓜ Baroque monuments　　Ⓢ Noble sweetness

GLOSSARY

The language of wine

Aroma
The entirety of the substances that gives each wine its typical scent and flavor.

Astringent
Extremely dry, constricting or furry feeling on the palate, elicited by too high a level of acidity or of tannins.

Base wine
Fermented wine, from which sparkling wine is developed during the second fermentation.

Böckser
Collective German term for wine faults (meaning 'goaty smell'), usually the formation of hydrogen sulfide, noticeable via the smell of bad eggs and/or sulfur. Slight occurrences of böckser may disappear through aeration of the wine.

Botrytis
A form of vine rot occurring when the fungus *Botrytis cinerea* affects ripe, undam-aged grapes with its enzymes and perforates the grape skins. In favorable warm and dry weather conditions, over half of the fluid stored in the grapes evaporates, and at the same time the concentrations of sugar and aromas increase. The botrytis fungus produces a number of chemical compounds, such as glycerine, gluconic acid and aroma agents such as sotolon.

Canopy management
Intentional control and shaping of canopy growth in order to achieve optimum shading, aeration and light, as well as the rapid drying of leaves and grapes.

Conversion of measurements
1.00 (US) gallon = 3.79 liters
1.00 liter = 0.26 (US) gallons
1.00 mile = 1.6093 kilometers
1.00 kilometer = 0.6214 miles
1.00 foot = 0.3048 meters
1.00 meter = 3.2808 feet
1.0 acre = 0.4047 hectares
1.0 hectare = 2.4711 acres

Cool fermentation
Temperature-controlled fermentation in order to reduce the warmth arising from the fermentation process itself and thereby retaining the lacy, primary fruit aromas in the resulting wine.

Cover crop
Permanent or seasonal covering of the soil between the rows of vines via sowing or natural growth of vegetation, for example grass. Above all, species-rich mixtures with clover and herbs are preferred in organic wine growing.

Cultured yeasts
Selected yeast strains from successful spontaneous fermentation which, as cultured yeasts, consist of 100% *Saccharomyces cerevisiae* and can be added to the must in the form of dried yeast cultures.

Enrichment

Strictly controlled in Germany since the introduction of the wine laws in 1971: in principle, the addition of sugar is forbidden, the sole exception being the sweetening (chaptalization) of Q.b.A. wines before fermentation, in order to increase subsequent alcohol levels.

Fermentation

Alcoholic fermentation is the transformation of sugar into alcohol and carbon dioxide. It is triggered by yeasts which are present in the grapes in a natural form or which are added to the must in the form of cultured yeasts.

Green harvest

Intentional cutting away of the still unripe green grapes – as a rule about mid-August in the northern hemisphere – in order to increase the concentration of flavor in the grapes remaining on the vine. In contrast to red wine varieties, the green harvest has not become particularly established with Riesling grapes.

INAO

Institut National des Appellations d'Origine. This organization is in charge of the administration, regulation and granting of the Appellations contrôllées in France. Along with wine, the organization's authority covers also spirits, cheese and other foods, and drinks. The INAO was founded as early as 1935.

Malolactic fermentation

In malolactic fermentation, malic acid, which naturally occurs in wine, is transformed by lactic acid bacteria into milder lactic acid, thereby setting free carbon dioxide. The reduction of acidity leads to a change in the aroma and fruit intensity. If the malolactic fermentation is interrupted before the transformation of malic acid is complete, then unpleasant aromas may arise in the wine which are reminiscent of yogurt, cheese or whey, or in extreme cases even of sauerkraut.

Minerality, mineral

A term addressing the flavor of wine, describing the lightly salty aroma and flavor notes which are above all reminiscent of slate. In addition it is considered as a criterion for terroir-based wines and as a synonym for flavoral elegance.

MW (Master of Wine)

The title Master of Wine is the best-known and most highly respected qualification in the wine business. The title is conditional on passing the examination, held annually by the Institute of Masters of Wine in London. Today there are 248 Masters of Wine worldwide and 58 of these are women. The MW examination requires a broad knowledge of enology and winemaking on an international basis. Additionally, special expert knowledge is required about such themes as marketing, trade quality control and commercial aspects of the wine business as well as general wine-knowledge and excellent degustation expertise.

Oxidative treatment

A method of treatment by which the must comes into contact with oxygen during fermentation. Oxidation of the individual components of the wine is desired during ripening and aging, which is intentionally induced via storage in wooden vats or barrels.

Recipient

A container for the processing, aging and storage of wine, for example oak vats, fiberglass or stainless steel tanks and carboys etc. Regarding the volume of containers, one speaks of cask size.

Reductive treatment
A processing method by which the chemical reactions of fermentation occur under airtight conditions – for instance in steel tanks – in order to produce particularly fresh and fruity wines with a singular tone.

Residual sugar content
Sugar from the grapes which is not transformed into alcohol as a result of an intentional or spontaneous termination of the fermentation process. The residual sugar content is declared in grams per liter.

Ried (plural: Rieden/Riedel)
Common term for a wine site in Austria, in Austrian German.

Seasoned oak
A term describing the wood used in a wine barrel or vat which, before it is used for the first time, is prepared with water or steam so that possible undesired flavoral components are removed from the wood.

Single vine training
A regional form of vine training which is practiced above all on extremely steep sites such as in the Mosel region. A single vine is trained on each post, and the vine's bearers as well as its shoots and canes are tied to it. A steep vineyard can be easily accessed at right angles to the slope via single vine training.

Sour rot
Fungal disease occurring in unripe grapes.

Terroir
French word for earth/soil, but used in the wine world as a term for the interplay of natural and cultural parameters in the creation of a wine.

Training system
The training of vines and their growth form, for example via supporting systems. The choice of the form of training depends above all on the geological and climatic conditions in the vineyard but also on the rate of growth of the vine. Today, because of the financial constraints affecting winemaking, training systems are often preferred if they allow mechanization in the vineyard.

Wingert
Common term in some German regions for a vineyard (usual term: Weinberg).

Whole-bunch pressing
A pressing technique by which the grapes are promptly pressed without previous mechanical processing or maceration time after harvesting. It is above all applied in order to produce fruitily-elegant and pure-toned white wines. However, this pressing method can lead to a deficit in the substance of the wine and its storage ability, since the majority of aromas are present in the grape skins and are not released by whole-bunch pressing.

Yeast types
Wild yeasts, also known as spontaneous yeasts, are naturally occurring yeasts in the must. 90% of spontaneous yeasts are so-called apiculatus yeasts which are not suited to complete fermentation and can introduce undesirable flavor-forming characteristics into the wine such as ethyl acetate, volatile acidity and hydrogen sulfide (böckser), smelling of bad eggs.

INDEX

Quick reference

A last word on...

teamwork, the most important keyword: We would
therefore like to take this opportunity to sincerely
thank Prof. U. Fischer, Marc Strittmatter, Eva Meyer,
all the wine makers and above all those dear individuals
who stood steadfastly by us during these last months
and patiently answered question upon question.

Ingo Swoboda and Christina Fischer

Photographs: Robert Dieth p. 2, 6, 8, 11, 12/13, 15, 18,
20, 21, 22, 24, 25, 26, 28, 30, 32, 33, 34/35, 46, 49, 55, 79,
88, 89, 96, 97, 98, 104, 105, 106, 107, 108, 112, 113, 114,
115, 116, 117, 122, 123, 124, 125, 129, 132, 133, 135, 144,
145, 146, 147, 148, 164, 166; Stefan Braun p. 76/77, 80,
81, 82, 83, 84, 85, 86, 87, 92/93, 94, 102, 110, 120, 130,
140, 150/151, 153, 154; Sabine Jellasitz p. 57, 61, 118,
127, 136, 137, 139; Cephas/Kevin Argue p. 67;
Cephas/Juan Espi p. 75; Cephas/Mick Rock p. 51, 71;
Corbis/Charles O'Rear p. 40; Alfred Ernst p. 163;
Harald Rüssel p. 160; Teubner Foodfoto GmbH p. 161.

Sources of national statistics (pp 39–75): Excerpt
from the report on the worldwide wine economy 2003,
presented by Frederico Castellucci, general director of
the O.I.V. 2004, on the occasion of the XXVIII World
Congress in Vienna. Figures from 2002
www.oiv.int

The publishers wish to thank the following
institutions for their support in realizing this book:

Deutsches Weininstitut GmbH
www.deutscheweine.de

VDP. Die Prädikatsweingüter
www.vdp.de

Publishing director: Dorothee Seeliger
Project manager and editor: Marc Strittmatter
Picture editing and editing assistance: Dagmar Reichel
Cover design and interior layout: Büro für
KommunikationsDesign Jorge Schmidt, Munich
Production: Markus Plötz

English edition produced by:
Werkstatt München · Buchproduktion, Munich
Translation: Jon Smale, Munich
Copy editor: Michael Scuffil, Cologne
Managing editor: Martin Waller, Munich
Composition: Anja Dengler, Munich

Repro: Fotolito Longo, Bolzano, Italy
Printing: Firmengruppe APPL, aprinta druck,
Wemding, Germany
Binding: Firmengruppe APPL, m. appl,
Wemding, Germany

Maps : © MERIAN-Kartographie, iPUBLISH GmbH,
Munich

HALLWAG is a member of the
GRÄFE UND UNZER VERLAG GmbH, Munich,
GANSKE VERLAGSGRUPPE

leser-service@hallwag.de
www.hallwag.de

ISBN: 978-3-8338-0986-6

Ein Unternehmen der
GANSKE VERLAGSGRUPPE